Machine Patchwork
technique and design

Dorothy Osler

B T Batsford Ltd London

Filmset in 'Monophoto' Apollo by
Servis Filmsetting Ltd, Manchester
Printed in Great Britain by
The Anchor Press Ltd, Tiptree, Essex
for the publishers
B T Batsford Ltd
4 Fitzhardinge Street
London W1H 0AH

Acknowledgme

I wish to thank the following for permission to reproduce photographs of their work: Dierdre Amsden for figures 11, 35 and 36, Pauline Burbidge for figures 39, 40 and 41, Barbara Robson for figures 31 and 32 and Eng Tow for figures 30, 37 and 38. I wish also to thank the following for permission to photograph their work: Janet Jacobson for figures 20, 33, 34 and 65 and Diane Marshall for figure 63.

I wish to thank the following for permission to reproduce works in their collections: Beamish, North of England Open Air Museum for figures 1, 2 and the colour plate facing page 72, Durham County Council (Bowes Museum) for figure 5, Victoria and Albert Museum, London for figure 6, Norfolk Museums Service (Strangers Hall Museum, Norwich) for figure 35, Diane Marshall for figures 7, 8 and 10 and Rosemary Blackett-Ord.

I acknowledge with gratitude the help received from Rosemary Allen of Beamish, North of England Open Air Museum, Caroline Fielding of the Quilt Circle, John Millard and Lesley Forster of Tyne and Wear County Council Museum Service (Shipley Art Gallery, Gateshead) and Frister and Rossman Sewing Machines.

The photographs of my own work and that lent to me for reproduction were taken by Jeff Maughan, Newcastle on Tyne. Photographs 31 and 32 are by David Hastey, Halifax, Nova Scotia, and 11, 35 and 36 by Dona Haycraft, Cambridge.

I would also like to thank Joan Batey for typing the manuscript and my sister, Maggie Cullen, for modelling the clothes. Last, but certainly not least, I wish to thank my husband, Adrian, for his tireless efforts in providing the illustrations.
Newcastle upon Tyne 1980   D O

Contents

1 Quilt in a *Basket* pattern with strips separating the plain and patchwork blocks. Made in 1912 of pink and white cotton with the patchwork pieced by machine and the basket handles appliquéd by hand. The hand-quilting is known to have been done by Mrs Adamson of Rookhope, County Durham, and the design marked by Elizabeth Sanderson, a noted quilt-marker

Introduction

There is no doubt that interest in patchwork is growing rapidly – articles and illustrations are appearing with increasing frequency in magazines, books on the subject are in constant demand from libraries, and programmes on patchwork are appearing on our television screens. Touring exhibitions of patchwork quilts in museums and galleries up and down the country are proving enormously popular. Suddenly, two or three generations of women (and hopefully, men) are coming into contact with a craft about which, hitherto, they have known little.

Patchwork is not alone among crafts in enjoying this revival. Handicrafts of all kinds are becoming increasingly popular, including knitting (for too long considered the preserve of granny in her rocking chair), which has taken on a new respectability as a craft.

Why the sudden boom? One obvious factor is the increased leisure time available either through shorter working hours or, in the case of the housewife, the widespread use of labour-saving devices in the home. But it also seems that many people are discovering the satisfaction and relaxation that working with their hands can bring. They are discovering the pleasure and sense of achievement which comes from making something entirely by themselves, using skill and ingenuity and exercising individual taste in colour and design. Many of us feel a need just to make things – a need to be creative. Before the Industrial Revolution, making things for domestic and personal use was part and parcel of everyday life among ordinary folk. Today, everything we need we can go out and buy but much of it is cheap and tawdry and often the feeling that 'I could do better myself' is sufficient to make someone turn to doing just that.

So, if interest in craftwork in general is growing, what has patchwork in particular to offer? First of all, it needs no special equipment beyond the normal sewing items found in most homes. Secondly, the techniques used are not difficult, particularly for experienced dressmakers or needlewomen. Thirdly, it offers the opportunity to explore pattern, texture and colour and, at the same time, make attractive and useful things for the home, for friends or for your wardrobe. All in all, it is an easy craft to take up and it offers almost limitless possibilities for individual interpretation.

Also, for many people, it has one additional appeal – it provides an opportunity to use up old discarded clothing, dressmaking left-overs, jumble sale bargains and other fabric scraps. It can be an economy craft. Often old clothes are retained for their sentimental value – one elderly lady told me she had saved all her daughter's cotton dresses and stored them in her attic. When she was tied to the house nursing a sick relative, she brought down the dresses and passed the time making them into patchwork curtains. She told me, 'It was such fun to piece my memories together'.

2   Medallion-style quilt in cotton with a central square of checked
printed cotton. This quilt is typical of the Northern England
medallion-style quilts with alternate plain and patchwork borders
but this one was pieced by machine probably in the early 1900s

6

So patchwork has much to commend it as a hobby or pastime. It therefore seems a pity that, despite the increasing popularity of the craft, so many people remain unaware that sewing machines can be used for patchwork. Many people say to me, 'I thought you had to do it by hand'. In many cases, it is just as easy to sew patches by machine as it is by hand and, certainly, a good deal quicker.

Machine patchwork is not, however, without its critics. I have been told that 'It isn't traditional' and 'It's cheating' and even that 'It's a corruption of the art'. The staunchest traditionalists on this side of the Atlantic tell me that I must over-sew my patches together with 16 stitches to the inch – they have not worked out how many to the centimetre yet!

These criticisms are based on ignorance of the history of patchwork and its techniques. Patchwork was sewn by hand largely because there was no alternative. As soon as sewing machines became widely available they were used for piecing patchwork. There is ample evidence for this. Museum collections in the United States and Canada contain a number of patchwork quilts pieced by machine towards the end of the nineteenth century. Here in England, I have found two splendid patchwork quilts, pieced by machine and quilted by hand, in the collections of the North of England Open-Air Museum at Beamish in County Durham. They were both made around 1910. The piecing is careful and accurate and the quality of the work is every bit as good as those quilts pieced by hand. Indeed, these two quilts are two of the better examples of patchwork in the Beamish collection which may suggest that those workers, well-practised and skilled in the craft, recognised the potential of the machine for patchwork even then. However, patchwork was already well on the decline by that time in Britain, so the idea of using sewing machines never had much chance to become widely established.

In North America, machine-sewn patchwork is more widely accepted. There are probably two historical reasons for this. Firstly, the method of hand-sewing patchwork by tacking each patch over a paper pattern and over-sewing the patches together (sometimes called the 'English' method) was less common in America than in Britain. Instead, the American women sewed their patches together with a running stitch forming an ordinary flat seam. This, the so-called 'American' method, was much easier to translate onto the machine. It was a simple and logical step to replace the running stitch with a row of machine stitching.

Secondly, making patchwork quilts never declined to the extent it did here in Britain nor did patchwork and quilting diverge so much. Patchwork in North America had a much broader base at the turn of the century and therefore much greater scope for trying the new machine-sewing technique.

The great advantage of machine patchwork is its speed and the strength of its stitching. Cushions can be made in an evening, quilts in a week or two. The traditional patterns which our great-grandmothers laboured over through the long winter's nights can now be pieced together in a few evenings. However, there are disadvantages. The work is not so portable, nor can we sit in an armchair to do it. Some designs are not so easily pieced by machine – patterns which have curved seams or pieces which fit into a sharp angle are tricky and best avoided by the beginner. However, more of this in a later chapter.

The purpose of this book is to show that machine-sewn patchwork is a perfectly valid alternative to hand-sewn patchwork. I hope, also, to show some of the great variety of patterns which can be pieced together by the machine and the many uses which can be made of patchwork, and some of the beautiful and exciting results which can be attained.

But first it is necessary to understand just how a piece of patchwork can be planned, cut out and put together. For this reason, the first part of the book describes, in general terms, all these working stages. The second part describes, in detail, how to make selected items which have been specifically designed to include a variety of patterns and methods. I hope that, through these, the reader can be introduced to different patchwork techniques and given the confidence or encouragement to take the craft further. I would stress, however, that machine patchwork is *not* a different craft from hand-sewn patchwork. It is simply a different method. So, much of what is said in this book is equally applicable to hand-sewn patchwork. Indeed, you can still follow all the instructions if you want to hand-sew and merely replace the machine stitch with a running stitch or embroidery stitch, whichever is applicable.

Finally, I would emphasise that a good piece of patchwork is a careful combination of colour, design and fabric together with fine workmanship. The care and thought which goes into all these aspects will be clearly reflected in the finished work and will repay all the time and trouble taken.

NOTE   All measurements in this book are given in metric with the imperial measurements in brackets alongside. The imperial measurements are not necessarily the exact equivalent but the nearest useful equivalent. If you are following instructions, follow *either* the metric *or* the imperial measurements but do not change from one to the other.

Patchwork — a short history

Patchwork is a domestic craft and, like many similar crafts, its origins are lost in antiquity. The earliest surviving examples are fragments of pieced silks and damasks found in India which date from the sixth and ninth centuries AD but records and illustrations show that patchwork was known in Ancient Egypt as far back as BC 1000. However, examples of early patchwork are very rare because textiles do not survive well.

The earliest surviving example of British patchwork is the set of bed furnishings at Levens Hall in Kendal, Cumbria, made there in 1708. This is a painstaking piece of work, well designed and pieced, with nothing about it to suggest a craft in its infancy. There must already have been a well-established tradition of patchwork design and technique by that time. About this we know very little, though it seems likely that both patchwork and quilting were brought to England in the period of the Crusades. Both crafts were put to good use to provide warm, economical bed-quilts by using fabric scraps for the tops, and sheep's wool as wadding for the quilts.

A number of other examples of British patchwork have survived from the early and mid-eighteenth century but these are relatively few compared with those which have survived from the late eighteenth and the nineteenth centuries. From these examples we can follow the popular trends in design and fabrics and also the methods of piecing. Throughout these two centuries patchwork was a popular craft in Britain. It was especially associated with making bed-covers but patchwork garments were also made as well as cushions, table covers and seat covers. Attractive cotton prints, especially Indian chintzes and calicoes, were available and were very suitable for patchwork. This helped the change from a purely scrap craft to one where more ordered designs were possible.

The patterns to be found in this eighteenth and nineteenth century British work are many and varied and certainly not restricted to the ubiquitous hexagon so frequently associated with British patchwork. It is possible to see the forerunners of so many of the American block patterns in this English work – *Jacob's Ladder, Flying Geese, Broken Dishes, Log Cabin, Big T, Churn Dash, Baby Blocks, Tree Everlasting, Variable Star* – all these, and more, can be seen in the quilts and coverlets of this period. They must surely represent the 'roots' of much American patchwork.

The patterns of these quilts and coverlets include one-patch patterns, block patterns and overall patterns like the medallion or framed ones (see page 19 for description of these terms). The framed designs were especially popular among the quilt-makers of Northern England. The central block would either be a patchwork pattern like a star block or, sometimes, a printed fabric pattern would be used (see figure 2). When block designs were made they were often small units and made in a combination of several different block patterns. One coverlet in the Victoria and Albert Museum is made up of over two hundred blocks representing sixty to seventy different block patterns and is dated as 1797.

Patchwork was made in Britain by both country women in the farms and villages and by the 'gentlewomen' of the middle and upper classes. The patchwork produced clearly shows their different needs and life-styles. Amongst ordinary folk, the great need was for warm bed-covers so patchwork quilts were made using materials to hand. It was also a family activity – young girls helped their mothers and grandmothers to sew the patches together and quilt whilst the men-folk helped make templates or even assisted with sewing. The patchwork patterns used by these country women were on the whole relatively simple. Only the very 'best' quilts, perhaps a bride's quilt, were made in the intricate manner so favoured by the ladies of the leisured classes. These country women usually cut out their patches and sewed them directly together without individual paper templates, using either a running stitch or oversewing one piece onto another.

3   Detail from a coverlet made in Yorkshire and dated 1799. The block patterns included in the design resemble the American *Jacob's Ladder* and *Shoo Fly* blocks though they are made in smaller pieces than is usual in the American quilts. These blocks are approximately 12.5 cm (5 in) square

Among the ladies of the leisured classes, patchwork became something of a social grace but they seemed less fond of quilting than their country cousins. Instead, these ladies pieced large coverlets in intricate designs of small pieces which must have taken months, even years to complete. Again, patchwork was a family activity though restricted in this case, to the ladies of the household. The famous quilt made by Jane Austen, her mother and sister, and now housed at the Austen's house at Chawton, Hampshire, bears witness to this. These 'gentlewomen' favoured the one-patch designs and small block designs which they pieced using a wide variety of fabrics, usually cottons. They produced elaborate and, often, over fussy patchwork.

From the mid-nineteenth century onwards, English patchwork declined and diverged up two rather blind alleys. On the one hand, the need for economy amongst the country women lessened especially as machine-made blankets became widely available. They either stopped making patchwork quilts altogether or, in the areas where the tradition of making quilts was strong, they poured their talents and creativity into quilting. Where patchwork was retained it was used to complement the increasingly elaborate quilting and was more restricted in colour and pattern. Nevertheless, some of this late nineteenth century patchwork is of a very high standard.

The Durham *Basket* quilt in figure 1 is a typical example of this simpler, but attractive, work which has much in common with the American style. Eventually, even this simple patchwork declined amongst these country women, in favour of the plain quilts or 'stripey' quilts with their long broad stripes of alternating fabrics.

It was left to the Victorian ladies to preserve the tradition of making intricate patchwork coverlets destined to become family heirlooms. They produced over-elaborate designs often in the silks, satins and velvets fashionable at the time. Crazy patchworks, *Log Cabins* and the *Baby Blocks* were amongst the popular patterns and numerous examples of this type of work have survived. They used the 'English' method of piecing — tacking the fabric around individual paper templates and over-sewing the patches together.

The early twentieth century saw patchwork almost die out in Britain. The elaborate designs and expensive materials so beloved of the Victorians fell out of fashion. Their time-consuming method of piecing held less attraction for women who were now enjoying greater freedom and greater opportunities for activities outside the home. Young women no longer took on the tasks performed by their mothers. Patchwork fell out of fashion and there, for the next fifty years, it stayed.

Patchwork designs and techniques were taken across the Atlantic to North America with the early settlers from both Britain and the Low Countries of Europe. Across the Atlantic the winters were generally harsher and the need for warm bedcovers greater, so making quilts became an essential part of everyday life for these early settlers. A further problem were the restrictions imposed by the British Government on the import and manufacture of textiles in these new colonies in an attempt to protect the British textile industry. Thus every scrap of useful fabric had to be hoarded. The earliest American quilts were true 'scrap-quilts' made from a random assortment of fabrics probably pieced in the crazy quilt style. Gradually, as textile restrictions eased, ordered patterns became possible. At first, the patterns and techniques were, no doubt, based on those in practice in Europe – the appearance of so many identical patterns on both sides of the Atlantic must surely testify to that. But gradually the American women developed their own style – a simpler, bolder style which they combined with an imaginative use of colour and proportion. In particular, they adapted the block system of piecing patchwork and developed the technique of repeating a single block to produce an overall pattern effect much further than had been achieved in British patchwork. A great variety of new block patterns evolved, each with its own name according to locality. These names often reflect the environment and the important influences on the lives of those colonial women – *Log Cabin, Pine Tree, Wild Geese, Indian Hatchet, Crown of Thorns* are but a few examples of this.

The hundred years or so between the mid-eighteenth century and the mid-nineteenth century are generally accepted as the hey-day of both American and British patchwork. But it is also generally accepted that the patchwork quilts produced in America at that time achieved much greater heights of creativity and originality than their British counterparts, and showed a very high standard of workmanship. These quilts are rightly regarded as a true American folk-art representing an individual style developed and enhanced from its original European 'roots'.

Making patchwork quilts was also an important social activity amongst the settlers of North America. It may be this factor which held the two crafts of patchwork and quilting so closely together in the New World. Quilting parties or 'bees' were important social occasions, especially in isolated rural areas. A patchwork top would be pieced by one woman and, perhaps, her family then the neighbours were invited to help quilt the top. It was a grand self-help scheme and it gave the women the opportunity to dress up, have a day out and exchange gossip as they worked around the quilting frame. A whole folk-lore grew up around the making of patchwork quilts and the surviving quilts are a testimony to the spirit of the women who made them and the importance they attached to this expression of their skills.

The history of the development of American patchwork is a fascinating one and is now well documented in the many books which have been written in recent years. The livelier state of the

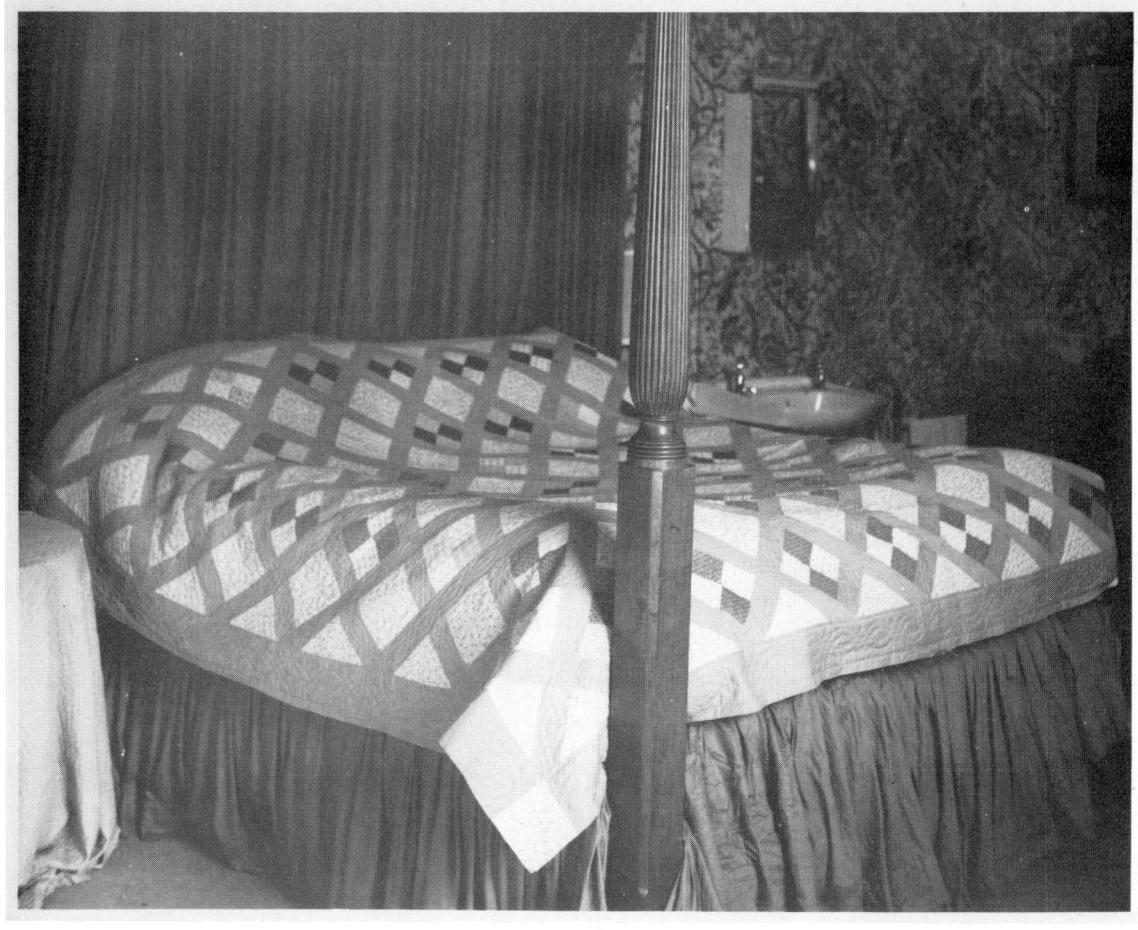

4 Quilt in alternate plain and four-patch blocks separated by
lattice strips and finished with border strips and corner squares.
This fine example of North-Country patchwork and quilting was
made in 1868 in Allendale, Northumberland – a noted centre of
country quilt-making at that time. It is pieced in cotton prints with
pink lattice strips and borders

craft helped the tradition to survive better than in Britain and,
when interest was renewed, there was still a strong folk memory
on which to build.

Interest in patchwork has revived strongly in both Britain and
North America since the early sixties. In the United States, in
particular, this interest is very strong and well organised.
Specialist books and magazines are readily available together with
shops catering for the needs of the patchworker and quilter.
Workshops, competitions and conventions add to the stimulus. In
North America, patchwork and quilting are still closely allied and
the emphasis very much on making quilts. Indeed, the word
'quilt' usually means a patchwork quilt. Sewing machines are

13

14

6 American coverlet pieced in the mid-nineteenth century. This
Pineapple pattern is found in nineteenth century work on both sides
of the Atlantic

◀ 5 Detail from mid-nineteenth century English coverlet pieced
mainly in satins. This one-patch pattern is known in America as
Broken Dishes

7   Crazy patchwork coverlet made in Missouri around 1880 by
Melinda Dawson Gray and typical of its period. The plain fabric
patches are embroidered along the edges and further embroidery
decorates almost every patch

16

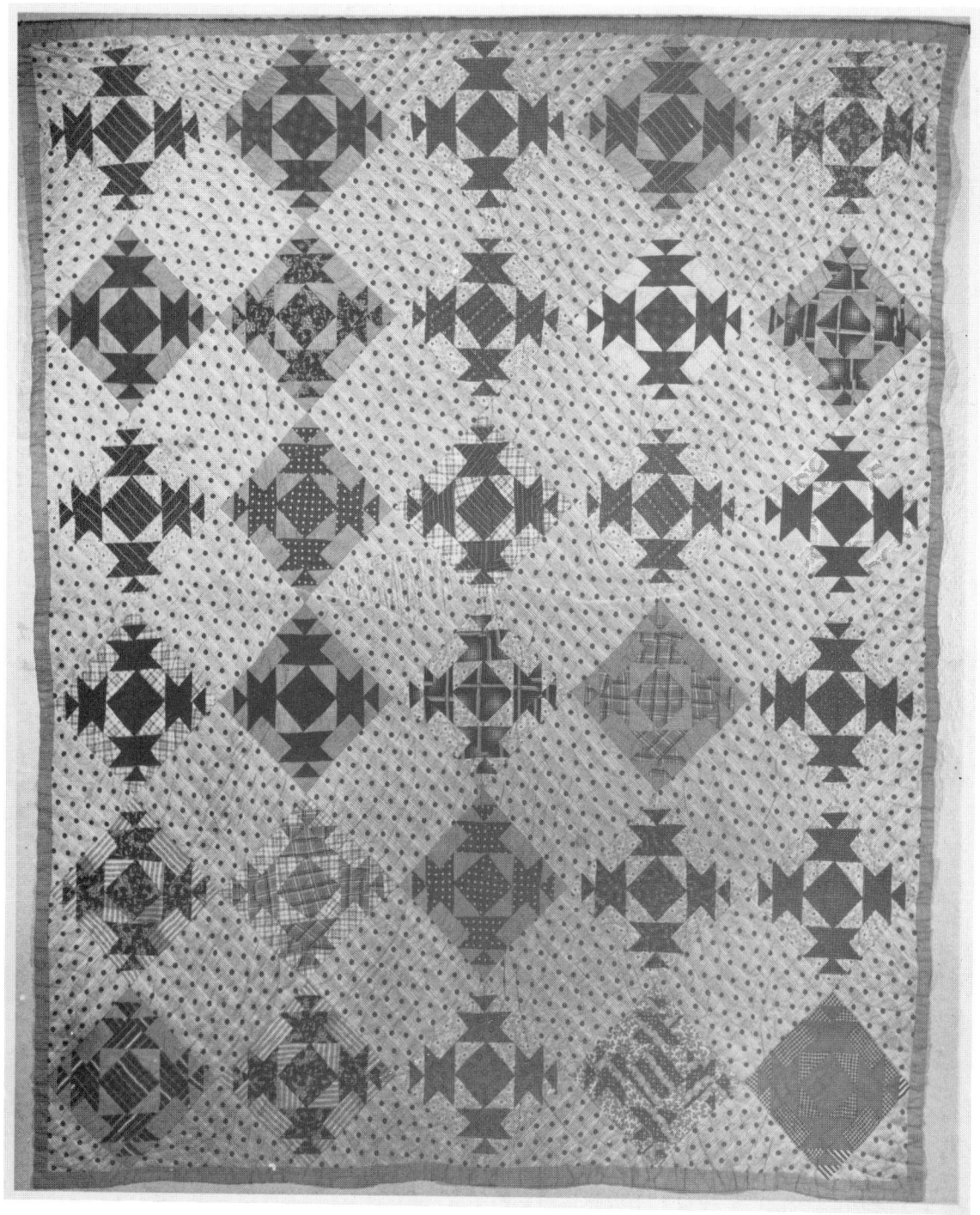

8 American block quilt with alternate plain and patchwork blocks
set on the diagonal. Made in Missouri at an unknown date, the
pattern is probably a Missouri variation of *Corn and Beans*

widely used for piecing patchwork and for quilting, though hand quilting is still very popular.

In contrast, the British revival picked up where the Victorian ladies left off – oversewing small patches, frequently hexagons, by hand. Rumaging through a jumble sale for cotton prints, I was asked, 'Oh, do you want them for those hexagon things?' The sad fact is that the collective folk memory has lost in three or four generations, the knowledge of piecing together the patterns and styles common in the nineteenth century amongst ordinary folk. We must now look to books and magazines to pick up the designs and techniques formerly handed down from mother to daughter.

There is still, in Britain, less general interest in combining patchwork and quilting. Patchwork is done for its own sake to make cushions, wall-hangings, clothing and the popular patchwork bedspread. Perhaps this is due to a lack of knowledge about how to quilt and how quilting can give an extra dimension to the patchwork. I would encourage anyone to try quilting at least some patchwork but I regret that any description of this craft is beyond the scope of this book. I have however, included books on quilting in the bibliography and you will see that many of the examples of patchwork illustrated, both old and new, have also been quilted.

The signs for the future look very hopeful with exciting and original new work being produced on both sides of the Atlantic. An encouraging trend is towards using patchwork and quilting as a communal activity. It does look as though the revival of interest in patchwork is more than just a passing fancy.

Historically, in addition to the names which have been given to different patchwork patterns, different types of patchwork quilts have been given names to describe the manner in which they have been put together. Since some of these terms may not be familiar to the reader, I will describe them here. Bear in mind that one quilt could be described in more than one way, for example, a scrap quilt could also be a crazy quilt or a one-patch quilt. It may also help to make clear the distinction between patchwork, appliqué and quilting since the three crafts are often so closely associated.

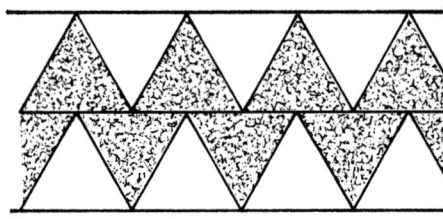

Half-lozenges (*Tumblers*)

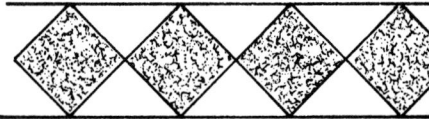

Squares and triangles

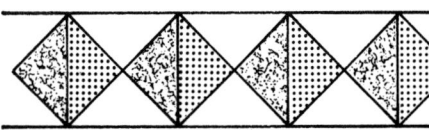

Triangles (*Broken Dishes*)

Rectangles and Triangles

Patchwork	sewing together small scraps of fabric (patches) to make a larger cloth. Patchwork is sometimes called *pieced work*.	**Terms**
Appliqué	sewing a small piece of fabric onto a larger piece of fabric. Sometimes called *applied work*.	
Quilting	stitching together three layers of fabric –	

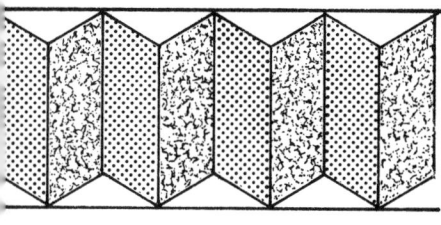

Rhomboids

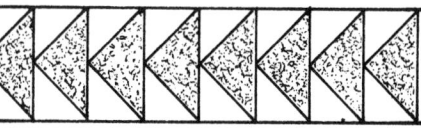

Triangles (*Goose-wing*)

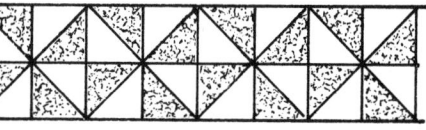

Triangles (*Windmill*)

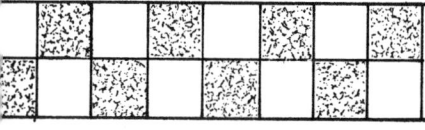

Squares (*Checkerboard*)

Border patterns

a top, a filling and a backing. The filling is usually soft wadding (known as batting in America).

Scrap quilt	made of a random assortment of fabric scraps which may or may not be in geometric shapes.
Crazy quilt	made of irregularly-shaped fabric scraps and usually pieced onto a foundation fabric.
One-patch quilt	the pattern is made up of one particular geometric shape only, eg hexagons, triangles, squares.
Medallion quilt	made up of a central 'medallion' or central block with a series of border strips with corner squares around this centre. The borders can be plain or a combination of plain and patchwork borders.
Block quilt	made of a series of patchwork units or blocks. These blocks are usually square but sometimes rectangular. They are usually repeated to produce an overall effect. The blocks may be set together with fabric strips, called *lattice strips* in between.
Friendship quilt	a block quilt where each block is made by a different person and often in a different pattern. The blocks in these quilts were usually set with lattice strips in between.
Album quilt	each block is a different pattern.
Strip quilt	the patchwork is either made in strips or grouped into long strip units, eg Tree Everlasting.
Pressed 'quilt'	the name, sometimes given to a 'quilt' made with the patches sewn onto foundation fabric. This style was frequently left unquilted because of the difficulties of working through an extra layer of fabric.
Strip patchwork	used to describe any patchwork where the basic fabric pieces are strips. Sometimes called *Log Cabin patchwork* but this more correctly describes a particular pattern.
Padded patchwork	used to describe patchwork which is padded or puffed either by sewing the patches directly onto wadding or by stuffing them individually.

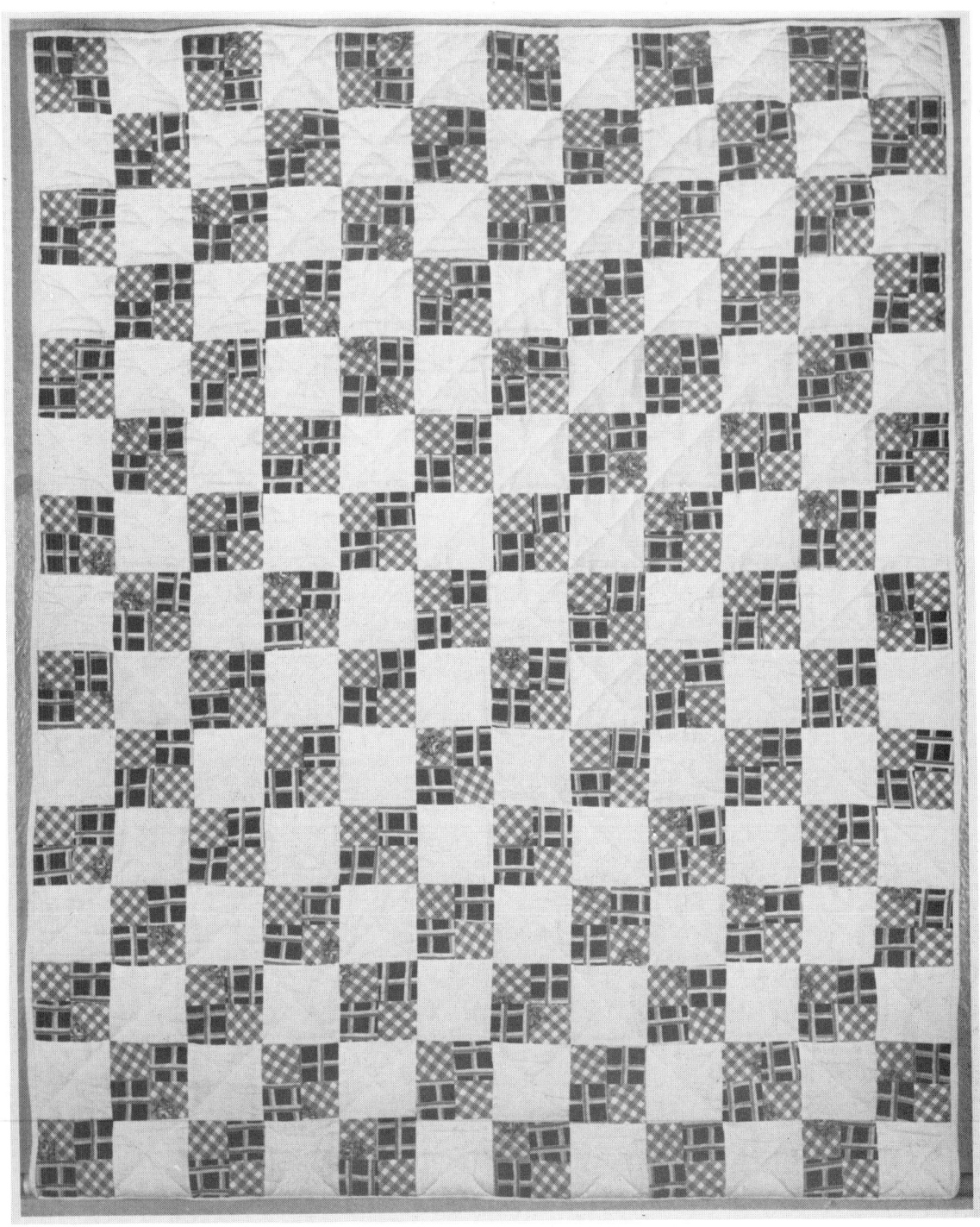

10   Cot quilt in alternate plain and patchwork blocks made by a
church quilting group in Missouri, 1976

11   Cot quilt in a *House* pattern made by Dierdre Amsden in blue,
navy, cream and green cottons

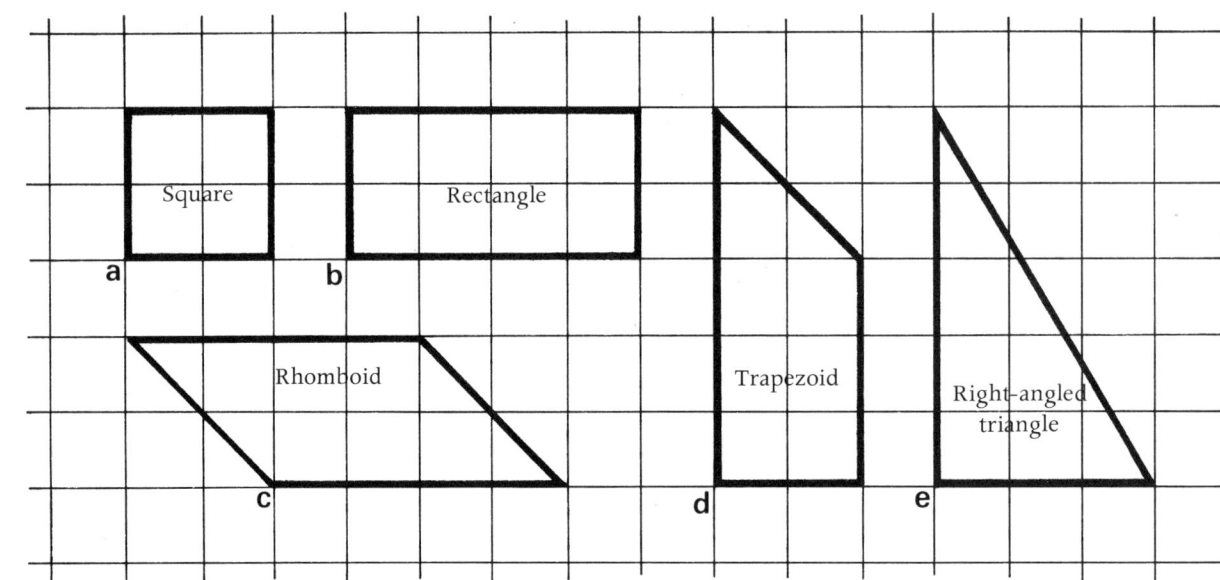

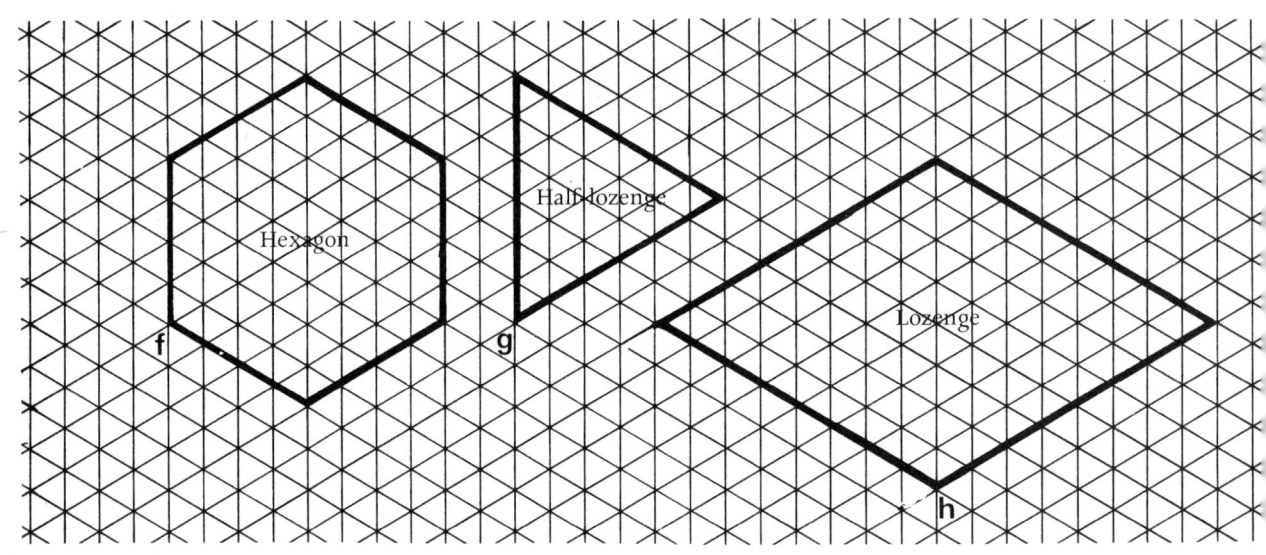

Triangular grid

12 Geometrical shapes commonly
used in patchwork on appropriate
graph paper

How to begin

Deciding what to make

Once you have made up your mind to try your hand – and machine – at patchwork, the first step is to decide what to make. Many people are drawn to patchwork by the beauty of patchwork quilts. Indeed, I was first inspired after seeing the beautiful quilts at the American Museum at Claverton Manor, Bath. But a full-size quilt or bedspread may seem too large a project to begin with, even if it remains an ultimate goal.

I would advise starting with something small, unless you feel very confident of your abilities to cope with a large project. Either a cushion (pillow, in American parlance) a cot quilt or a pram cover is a good 'starter'. All these items provide the opportunity to experiment with patterns, with different shapes and colours and to practise the techniques of machine patchwork. If you are pleased with the results then you can go on to produce something stunning on a larger scale. If not, well you have not wasted too much time or fabric and you can try again.

If you want to begin with something really simple, why not try some simple borders. These can be added to curtains, table covers, aprons and skirts – they are fun to do and can be very effective.

Do not be put off if your first effort is not a masterpiece. Very few of us master everything at the first attempt – you may find the techniques are relatively easy but you find more difficulty in combining colours and fabrics. Everyone has their own individual 'feel' for the colours and fabrics they like and it is very often a question of trial and error before you begin to see how you can combine these to your own particular satisfaction.

Measuring up

Before starting to make any piece of patchwork, it is important to know the final size you need for the article you are making. You should know this so that your finished piece of work will fit the purpose for which it is intended. I have seen beautiful patchwork cushions, for example, spoilt by being fitted with ill-fitting cushion pads and even if you are only making a small tea-cosy it would be a shame if, when you have finished, it did not quite fit your tea-pot.

So let us look at the measurements required for some of the popular patchwork items:

Quilts and bedspreads You will need to know the overall width and length required. The simplest way to acquire these measurements is to measure across and down the bed (with the bedclothes on) and include the amount you wish the spread or quilt to overhang the sides and front.

Duvet covers Duvets and duvet covers come in standard sizes (single, double and king sizes) so provided your duvet itself is a standard size, all you have to do is take the measurements from a plain cover, if you have one. If not, measure your duvet, and make your cover slightly smaller – 2.5 cm (1 in) less overall. In other words, take 2.5 cm (1 in) off the length of the duvet, and 2.5 cm (1 in) off the width.

Cushion covers   A cushion cover needs to fit snugly over the pad otherwise it will look too baggy or too tight and spoil the effect of the patchwork. To achieve a snug fit, the cover should be made just slightly smaller than the pad – about 2 cm ($\frac{3}{4}$ in) smaller overall. Do *not* make a cushion cover to a notional size then hope to go out and buy a pad to fit it. You will have great difficulty. Either make or buy your pad first, or use an existing one, and design your cover to fit.

Once you have obtained your basic measurements, you can then plan your design to fit.

Tools and equipment

The tools required for patchwork can be divided into two groups – those required for designing and making templates and those required for sewing the patches together (piecing). When piecing patchwork by machine, the machine simply replaces a needle and thread.

For designing and making templates you will need:
Graph paper
Pencils and pencil sharpener
Ruler
Coloured pencils, crayons or felt tip pens
Sandpaper (medium grade) and/or cardboard
Pair of compasses
Glue
Perspex/sheet metal/plywood ⎱ if required
Hacksaw or metal shears ⎰
Set square ⎱ if required
Protractor ⎰
Scissors (not dressmaking scissors)

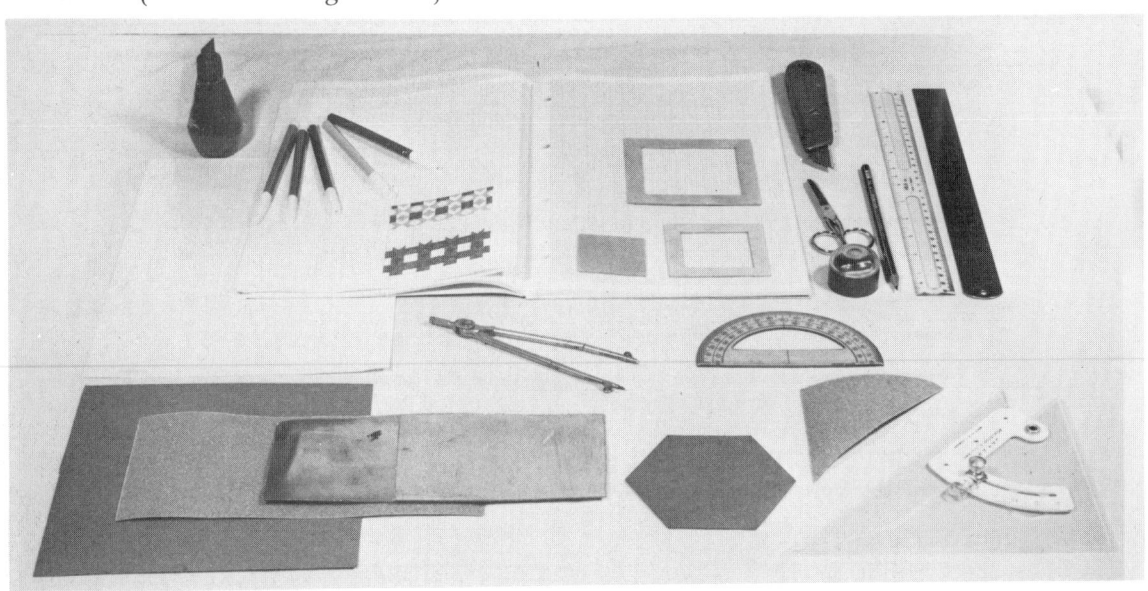

13   Tools and equipment for designing and making templates

Some readers may not be aware of the types of graph paper available. The most familiar and widely used is based on a square grid. The square grid may be divided into inches or divisions of inches, or centimetres or divisions of centimetres. A small grid (eg each square representing a millimetre) is best when using graph paper to draw out shapes for templates but a larger grid is preferable for drawing out complete designs. A less familiar type of graph paper is based on a triangular grid with all the triangles having equal sides and equal angles (60°). This graph paper is called isometric graph paper or Triangular Co-ordinate. It is extremely useful for drawing out designs based on hexagons, lozenges (wide diamonds), half-lozenges and for making templates of these shapes (see figure 12).

For cutting out, piecing patchwork and completing the work you will need:

Pins	Dressmaking scissors	Fabrics
Needles	Razor blade or seam ripper	Graphite pencil
Sewing threads	(for removing those seams	Chalk pencil
Sewing machine	that go wrong!)	Pencil sharpener
Tape measure		Iron

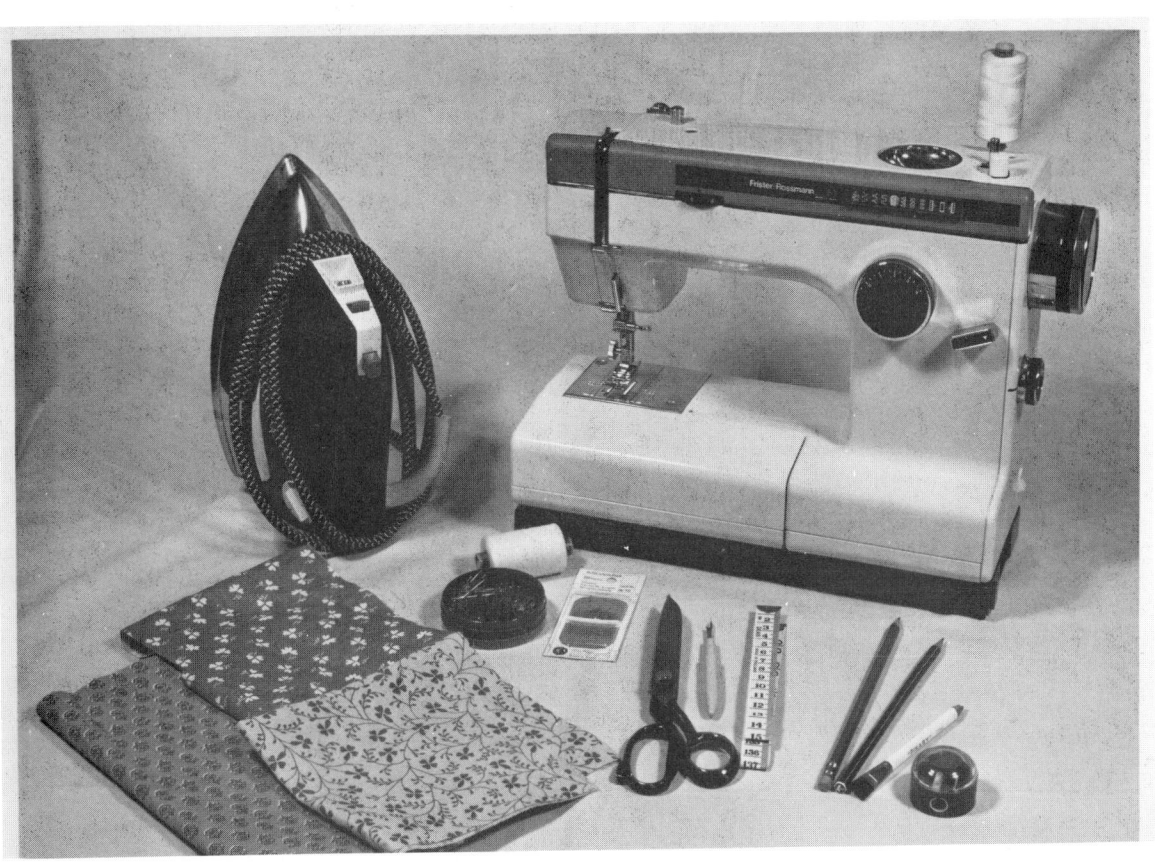

14 Tools and equipment for cutting out and piecing

Only the iron and sewing machine are expensive items of equipment but few homes are without an iron and many have a sewing machine.

The sewing machine itself deserves extra mention. A domestic sewing machine is, nowadays, a very sophisticated piece of machinery capable of doing a great variety of stitches. However, you do not need a very modern machine for patchwork. Any sewing machine can be used because the basic requirement is for the straight stitch that any machine can do. The old treadle machine on which I learnt to sew is still quite adequate for sewing patches together. But if you do have an up-to-date machine which will do a variety of stitches, then do experiment with it. Crazy patchwork, for example, was traditionally embellished with fancy embroidery stitches and the embroidery stitches on a modern machine could be used in much the same way (see also the Crazy Patchwork waistcoat in colour plate facing page 96).

Another item which deserves special mention is the sewing thread. The importance of using a suitable sewing thread is often overlooked but, after all, it is the means by which your patches are held together and, if it fails to do its job properly then your patchwork will fall apart. Patchwork, when sewn by hand, was originally sewn with linen thread but that was gradually replaced with cotton thread. Today, we also have polyester threads from which to choose. If you choose cotton thread, choose a good branded one. Cheap threads are often weak and rot easily when washed. I like to use polyester threads – I find them stronger and less likely to rot than cotton ones. However, there is a school of thought which says that cotton fabrics should always be sewn with cotton thread and polyester threads reserved for man-made fibres. It should also be remembered that polyester threads are relative newcomers to the market and may prove to have some disadvantages which only the test of time will show up. Whatever thread you use, you should try and match the thread to the colour of your fabrics. It is also much more economical to buy large reels of thread. The bedspread illustrated in colour plate facing page 73 used a mile of sewing thread, so buying in 100 m- (or 100 yd-) reels could prove quite costly.

Choosing a design and method

Choosing a design is the next logical step in making patchwork. In practice, this may be influenced by the fabrics to hand. There are three aspects to bear in mind when choosing a design for machine patchwork – the design should be functional, it should be attractive and it should be practically possible to assemble accurately by machine.

To be functional, the patchwork must fit the purpose for which it is intended. A simple tea-cosy should cover the tea-pot, keep the tea warm and be washable. It may be a beautiful and skilled piece of work but if it is not functional then it is badly designed.

15 Piecing triangles in the *Broken Dishes* pattern

The aesthetic aspects of design, the patterns which may be used and the ways they can be fitted together will be described in the next chapter, so let us go on to consider the practical aspects of piecing patchwork by machine and the methods which can be used. I will outline the methods here and describe them in detail in subsequent chapters.

Piecing shapes directly together

With this method, the fabric shapes are cut out using templates and sewn directly one to another using a flat seam (see figure 16a) or top-stitched together (see figure 16b). Each patch needs to be cut out individually before piecing.

Piecing shapes directly together is not difficult by machine provided you avoid the two main difficulties – curved seams and sharp-angled joins – until you have become very proficient. Avoiding sharp-angled joins is often a matter of working out the order for fitting your patchwork together beforehand. With a little thought it is usually possible to work out an order where all the pieces can be joined in straight-line seams. The simple pattern known as *Broken Dishes* illustrates this point (see also pages 74–76). If this is pieced in the sequence shown in figure 15a then the last triangle (4) has to fit into the angle between 1 and 3. If, however, the triangles are pieced as in figure 15b, with the

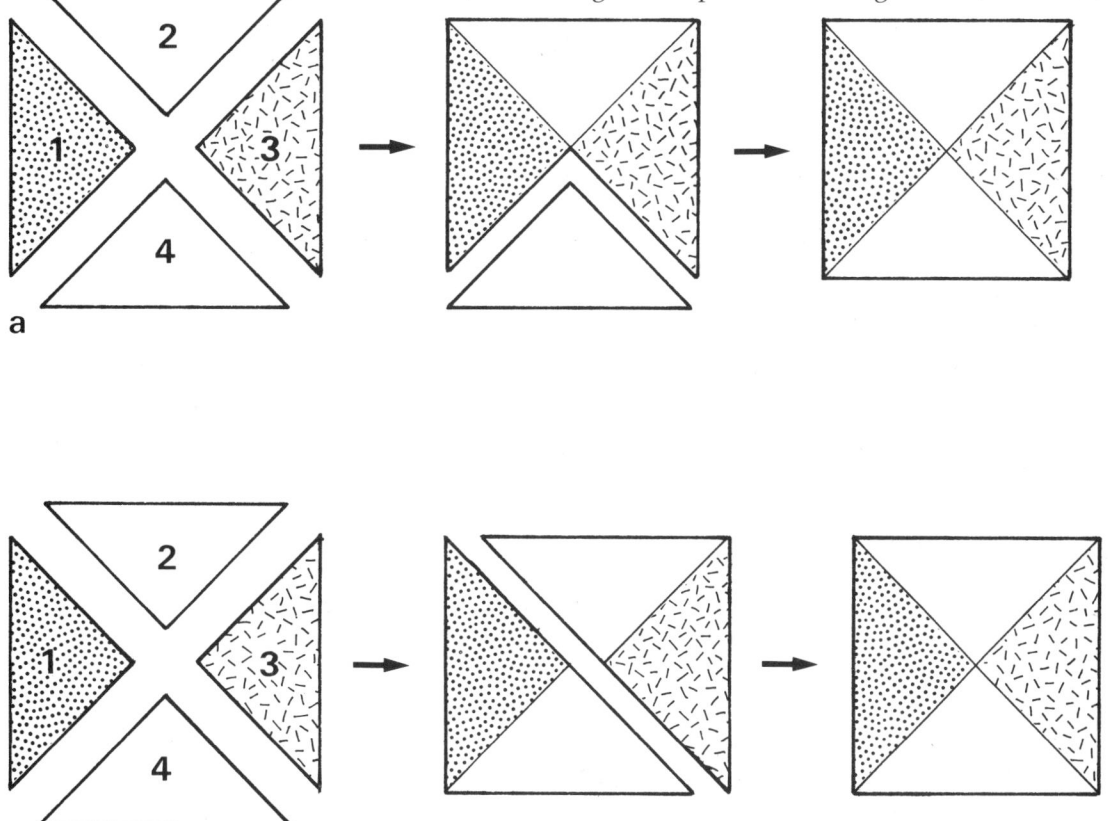

27

triangles joined first into pairs, then all the joins are simple straight-line seams.

There are also two variations on this basic method which are worthy of mention. The bedspread illustrated in figure 65 illustrates one of these. Long strips of the fabrics are first pieced together. These pieced strips, which can be made as long as possible from the fabrics available, are then cut into the required shapes (squares, triangles, etc) using large templates. These shapes are then pieced in the same way as shapes from single fabric. This method, a variety of *strip-patchwork* can be a quick and simple way of making very effective patchwork.

The second variation is known as *puff patchwork*. Puff patchwork is a special type of padded patchwork where the individual shapes are padded before being pieced together. This requires two fabric pieces for each shape, a front and a back, but the patchwork does not need lining and can be reversible.

16   Methods of machine-sewing patchwork
(a) Piecing geometrical shapes directly together with a flat seam

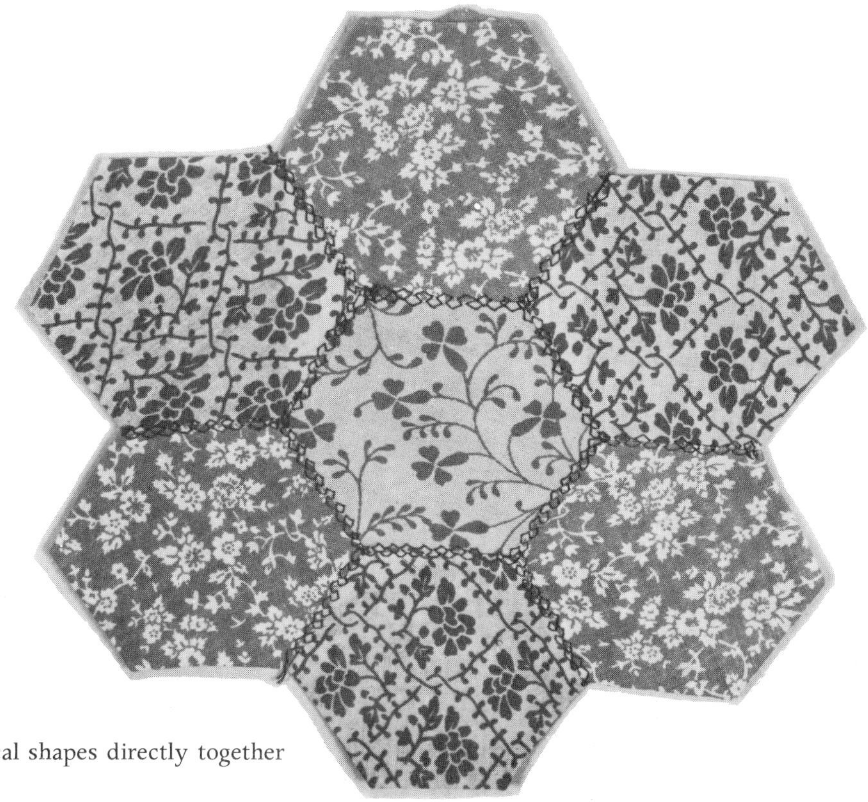

(b) Top-stitching geometrical shapes directly together

(c) Piecing onto foundation cloth

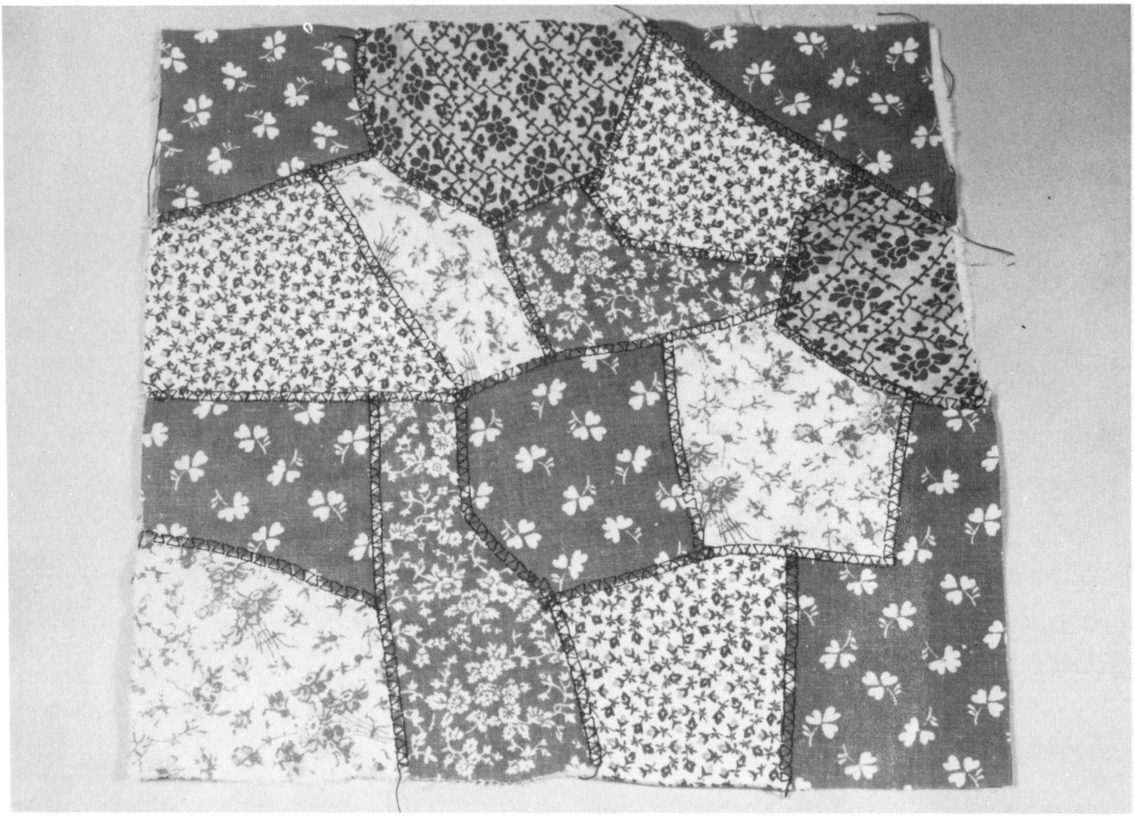

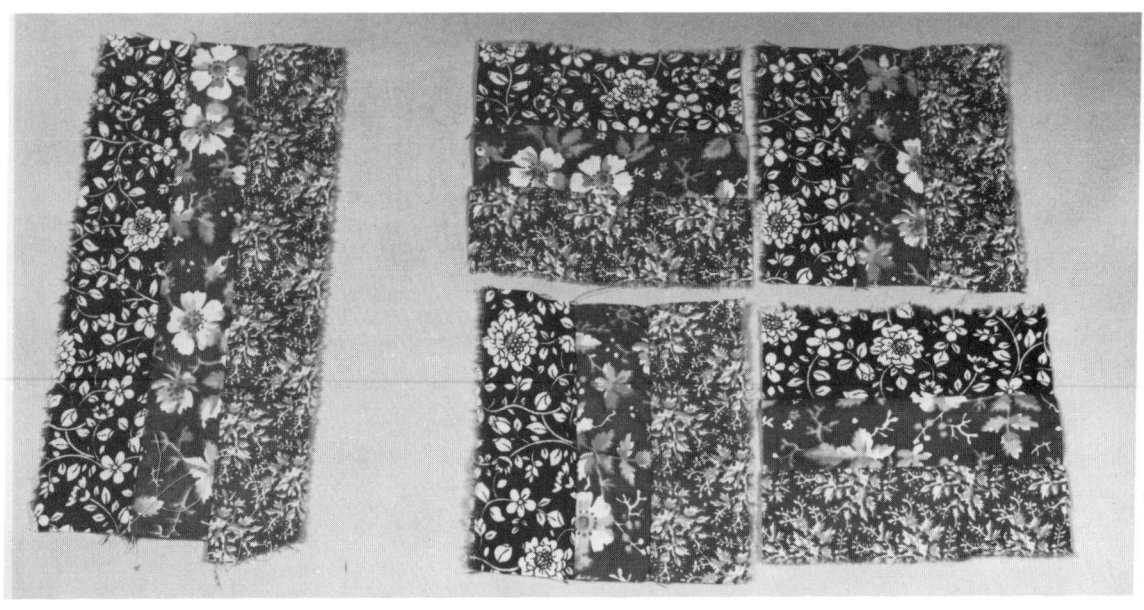

(d) Top-stitching onto foundation cloth

(e) Piecing strips then cutting into geometrical shapes

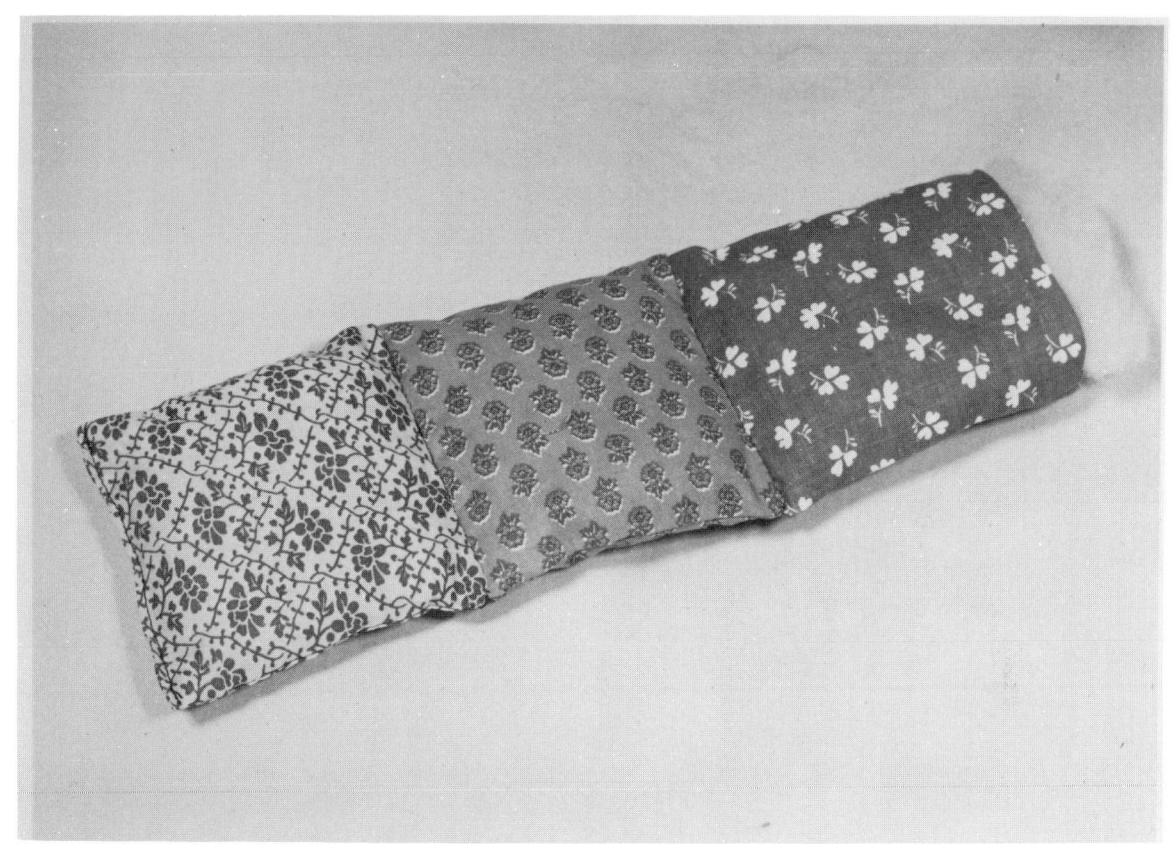

(f) Piecing together padded shapes (puff patchwork)

Piecing onto foundation cloth

Piecing onto foundation cloth requires the fabric patches to be sewn onto a base cloth (usually cotton fabric, eg calico) either with a flat seam (see figure 16c) or top-stitched one to another (see figure 16d). This method is most commonly used for *Log Cabin* patchwork and its variations and for Crazy patchwork.

The main advantage of this method is that less preparation time is needed before piecing because templates are not always needed and, for patchwork using strips, each piece does not have to be cut out separately. The fabric only needs to be cut out or torn into long strips, the longer the better. The speed and ease with which the strip designs like *Log Cabin* and *Courthouse Steps* can be pieced makes them very popular with newcomers to machine patchwork. In addition, this method of working produces a slightly raised patchwork which may be preferable if the patchwork is not to be quilted.

This method can also be used to produce a form of padded patchwork by using terylene wadding as the foundation cloth. The items illustrated in figure 17 have all been made in this way and the instructions given for the Crazy Patchwork Waistcoat (page 100) and the Tea-cosy (page 96) describe how this can be done.

17   Items made by piecing directly onto terylene (dacron) wadding

The main disadvantage of piecing onto foundation fabric is that it adds an extra layer of fabric to the work. This can add extra weight and may not be particularly suitable for something like a duvet cover. It also adds to the cost if you have to buy extra fabric.

32

Choosing fabrics

The fabrics which go into any piece of patchwork deserve a good deal of thought because they are the building blocks of which the patchwork is made. Fabrics come in a variety of textures, weights, patterns and colours and the qualities of the fabrics you use will be reflected in the finished patchwork. Choosing fabrics which will blend well together is not always easy and, in addition to ensuring that the fabrics chosen will blend together, you must also ensure they go together in practical terms, ie they can be washed or dry-cleaned together without disastrous results. If you want to go on to quilt your patchwork then that also must be considered in choosing fabrics.

Dress-weight cottons are much the easiest and most suitable fabrics to use for patchwork. They do not stretch or fray easily, can be folded and pressed down easily and, if you choose your patterns and colours with care, will look well together. A wide variety of dress cottons is available from which to choose, they are easy to wash and usually colour-fast but be wary of very fine cottons. They may be too flimsy and, if pale-coloured, the seam allowances may show through when pieced. It is, as a general rule, unwise to piece *any* fabric of different weights directly together because the heavy fabrics will pull and distort the lighter ones and may cause tearing.

Heavier-weight cotton fabrics such as gaberdine, denim, needlecord and corduroy are also used and can look very attractive. However, with needlecord, corduroy and also velvet, it is very important to keep the nap running in the required direction. The tone of the fabric hue will be affected by the way the light reflects on the nap so the same fabric can have a different appearance when the nap runs in an opposite direction.

Patchwork combining expensive fabrics like silks, satins and velvets was popular in Victorian times for use in the parlour as well as the bedroom. The rich quality of the fabrics can bring a beautiful, rich appearance to the patchwork but these fabrics are more difficult to work, more difficult to launder and may not wear well. Silk fabrics, in particular, do not stand up to the ravages of time – numerous examples of this Victorian patchwork have survived with the silks in tatters.

Nowadays, as well as the range of natural fabrics, we have a whole host of man-made fibres from which to choose, and with which to experiment. It is up to the individual to explore the possibilities of particular fabrics which appeal.

Obtaining fabrics

Most beginners to patchwork start by looking at their scrap bags, usually containing dressmaking left-overs and discarded clothes, to see what they can use. Patchwork, after all, began as an economy craft in this way. However, if you do this, select through your fabric scraps very carefully choosing patterns and colours which blend well together and complement your chosen design.

All too often, I find people try to combine all the pieces in their scrap bag and end up with a disappointing result.

A word of caution is appropriate here about using old fabrics. Material from old clothes, old household articles and jumble-sale bargains can frequently be put to good use in patchwork but it is wise to ask yourself how much useful life there is left in a piece of fabric. It seems a pity to spend a great deal of time on a piece of work which may disintegrate in a few washes. You may also find that old fabrics have faded and softened with washing and use. This can bring a charming soft and gentle look to patchwork when old fabrics are used together but when old and new fabrics are mixed, the effect is not always a happy one. Old fabrics can look very tired and jaded alongside new ones.

Sooner or later you will need to buy extra fabrics and will begin to scour the department stores and market stalls for suitable ones. Always take along samples of any fabrics with which you want new ones to blend – this is especially important when trying to buy suitable plain fabrics to co-ordinate with patterned ones. It seems many patchworkers main problem is trying to find suitable plain fabrics in appropriate colours. Some workers solve the problem by dyeing their own.

Some manufacturers do sell bundles of off-cuts and seconds as patchwork parcels'. With the exception of Laura Ashley parcels, I have not found these a very satisfactory purchase. Too often, they include fabrics and patterns not suitable for patchwork and, for every useful length, there is another one that ends up as a duster or floorcloth.

It is, however, useful to buy odd remnants, seconds or short lengths of suitable fabrics when you see them. You will soon come to know which fabrics and patterns are most suitable and which you like best, and if you buy them when you see them, you will build up a good stock of varied fabrics. This way, you may not have the problem of finding a good range of dress-weight cottons in winter and needlecord or corduroy in summer!

Preparation of fabrics

Whatever fabrics you choose they will need some preparation before you begin. All new fabrics should be washed to pre-shrink them and remove any sizing. Make sure you wash them at the appropriate temperature for the fabric. Fabrics should also be tested for colour-fastness, unless you are sure that the colour will not run, by leaving a swatch of the fabric soaking in warm water for about an hour. If you leave it in a glass bowl you can see at a glance if the colour of the water has changed. Some fabrics will run on the first wash but remain colourfast through subsequent washes so it is worth testing a couple of times on the same piece.

If you wish to remove the glaze from a glazed cotton or tone down a very bright colour, you can soak the fabric in hot water and bleach.

All fabrics should be carefully ironed before you proceed to cut out any patches.

Estimating fabric requirements

Working out how much fabric is needed *before* cutting out any shapes is *essential* if you are to avoid the disappointment of almost finishing your patchwork then finding you have run out of a crucial fabric.

Estimating the fabric required can only be done when you have chosen your design. If you are using a design with geometrical shapes, you need to count up how many patches are needed of each shape in the design. You can then work out what length of fabric is required for each shape.

For example, I have worked out a design which requires seventy two 7.6 cm (3 in) squares. To cut out the square I need a piece of fabric 9.5 cm ($3\frac{3}{4}$ in) square to include the seam allowance. From fabric 90 cm (36 in) wide I can cut nine squares across the width (see figure 18). If nine squares can be cut from one width 9.5 cm ($3\frac{3}{4}$ in) long, then I need seven further widths of that length to cut out the seventy-two squares. The total length I require is therefore 9.5 cm ($3\frac{3}{4}$ in) × 8 which equals 76 cm (30 in).

The length required for other shapes is worked out in the same way by deciding how many patches can be cut out along the width and then working out the total length required.

This method gives the length of fabric required if the fabric is all in one piece. If, however, you are using short lengths or scraps you will need to allow extra length to allow for wastage.

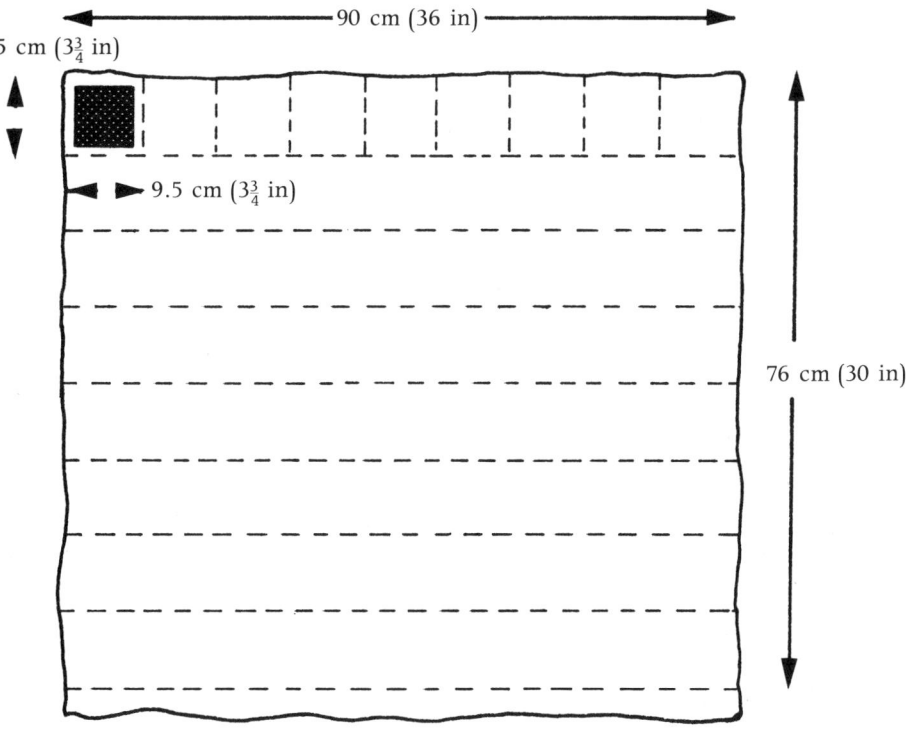

18 Estimating fabric length required for single shape

If you are not using a design with geometric shapes but a strip design, such as *Log Cabin*, the usual method is to measure the total length of strips required for one block or unit. Work out what length of fabric will be required to give this length of strip, assuming the strips are cut across the fabric width. Multiply this by the total number of blocks or units in the design to give the total length of fabric required.

Designing

Designing is, simply, planning a piece of work to ensure that the completed piece is both functional and aesthetically attractive. In patchwork, it means working out the overall size, the pattern, the colours, the textures and the proportions before you start to cut out and sew. It is perhaps the most important and often the most neglected aspect of patchwork.

Designing usually begins with some kind of mental image or idea – it may be a pattern image or a picture, a colour combination or a particular combination of pattern and colour. It may have come from something you have seen elsewhere, perhaps a traditional quilt pattern, or it may be your own original idea. This mental image then needs to be related to the item to be made and translated into a visual impression of the finished work. The simplest, effective way to create this visual impression is to make a scale drawing. At this drawing stage, you can experiment with sizes, shapes and colours selecting those you like and discarding those you do not. This scale drawing also has a very practical purpose – the final drawing will tell you how many patches of each shape, colour and fabric you will need and will act as a useful reference when you come to fit the shapes together. It is both a visual impression and a working diagram.

Before going on further, let me first reassure those readers who are already beginning to wonder if this aspect of patchwork is for them. In my patchwork classes, I find some students take quite happily to drawing out a design idea, others get very worried about it. They say, 'I can't draw' or 'I'm no good at art' – the labels they were stuck with at school in the days when art classes meant painting pictures. You do not need to be a good illustrator to draw out a patchwork design. What you need is to be able to draw outline shapes with a ruler and pencil, to colour them in and to work out some simple arithmetic. Many patchworkers, myself included, have had no formal art or craft training whatever.

Of course, patchwork was not always designed in this way. The colonial women of America worked out their patchwork designs by folding over pieces of paper into the various patterns. By taking a large square of paper to represent a block, it is possible to fold and re-fold it in a variety of ways to produce many different patterns. The shapes made by the paper can then be cut out and used as patterns for making templates. However, the American women also had the collective knowledge of several generations on which to draw. This 'folk memory' contained not only the traditional patterns tried and tested by generations but also how to work patterns in light and dark tones, what scale of patterns to use for a large quilt or a small cot quilt, how to use borders and all the other 'little' things which can make or mar a basically good design. They had, in fact, a design tradition – the result of a social process of trial, selection and rejection.

Britain, too, had a design tradition. Some British patchwork shows evidence of being very carefully worked out in terms of colour and pattern. But some of the simple one-patch designs and the medallion-style designs just grew out of the pattern idea in the mind of the maker and the size required. One-patch designs can be very simply put together just by making a number of the basic units, eg rosettes of hexagons, and piecing them together until the required size is reached. Many medallion-style quilts, obviously made as utility quilts, are very crudely put together and the incomplete shapes show all too clearly that little attempt was made to work out how to fit a particular pattern into the appropriate border.

It is possible to work much as the women did in the old days and simply translate the pattern idea straight into patchwork. I did this with the first *Pineapple* cushion I made several years ago, like the one illustrated in figure 85. However, it was three cushions later before I finally arrived at a satisfactory balance between the size of the centre, the surrounding pieces and the overall size of the cushion. Experimenting in this way can be expensive in both time and fabric. If I had drawn out the three possibilities beforehand, I would have seen immediately which one worked best.

So, planning your design carefully beforehand is well worth while. It is not difficult, it may save you some awful mistakes and it can be fun. But before drawing out the design, you must make some decision on your pattern, colours, texture and scale.

Pattern in patchwork is the shapes used in the work and the way in which they are combined. Sometimes this is described as the design but I have tried to use the word 'design' to mean the overall planning of the work for its appearance and for its use.

There are infinite possibilities for pattern in patchwork. Shapes, whether geometrical or irregular, can be combined in an endless variety of ways and even the same basic pattern can take on a different appearance according to the colours and fabrics used. Traditional patchwork patterns, both British and American, reflect the well-tried ways of combining geometrical shapes. Some of these patterns are also found outside patchwork in other decorative wares. For example, the *Bow Tie* pattern is a common simple tile pattern used in both floor and wall tiles.

Patchwork patterns can be loosely grouped into one-patch patterns, block patterns, strip patterns and overall patterns and I will attempt to describe them within these categories. However, bear in mind that a particular pattern can fall within more than one group. For example, the block pattern known as *Windmill Blades* (see figure 21) can also be classed as a one-patch pattern because it is made up of a single geometrical shape – the right-angled triangle.

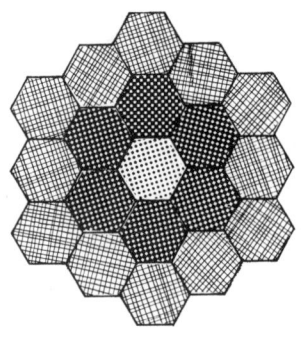

(a)   *Grandmother's Flower Garden*

Choosing a pattern

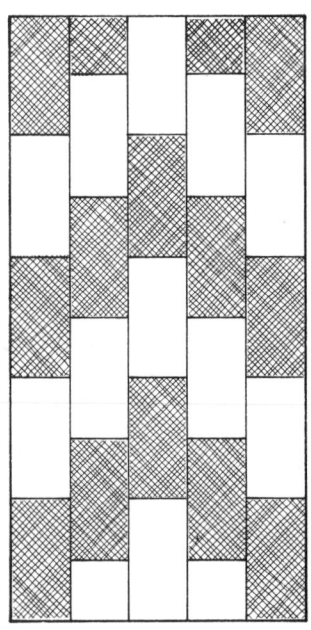

(b)   *Bricks*

38

(c) *Trip Around the World*

19a–c   Some one-patch patterns

One-patch patterns
The one-patch pattern, where a single shape of uniform size is used throughout, is the simplest form of patchwork pattern. The common shapes used for one-patch patterns are squares, rectangles, triangles and hexagons. Patterns using squares, rectangles and triangles are very simple to piece by machine but hexagons are difficult because, at some point, there is always a piece left to fit into a sharp angle. One way of overcoming this difficulty is to top-stitch hexagons together. This can look more attractive by using a decorative machine stitch rather than a straight stitch (see figure 16b).

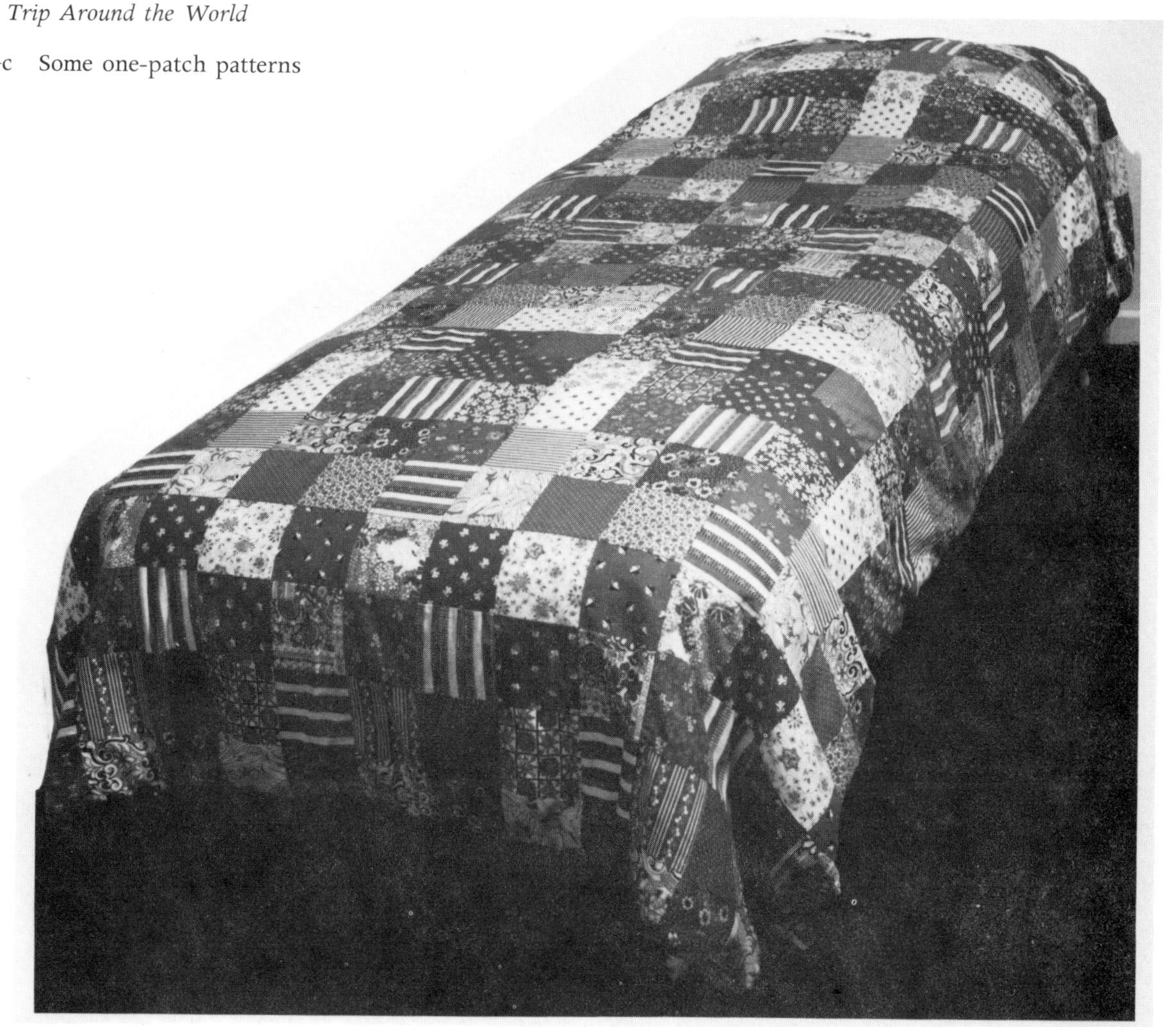

20   Bedspread in a random one-patch pattern of squares made by Janet Jacobson in predominantly red and blue cottons

Block patterns
A block pattern is made up of a series of units, usually square or rectangular, called blocks. Each block is made up of a particular arrangement of geometrical shapes. A block pattern can be the combination of a number of blocks of the same basic pattern or it can be the combination of different basic block patterns.

There are hundreds of known block patterns which, between them, use most of the common geometrical shapes – squares, triangles, rectangles, diamonds (both the long-diamond and lozenge), rhomboids and trapezoids. Hexagons are not a common element in block patterns. With the endless possibilities for creating pattern with shapes, it is also possible to create original block patterns. Any block pattern, either traditional or original, will create a variety of effects according to the fabrics used, the colours chosen and the manner in which it is joined to its neighbour.

The simplest block pattern is the *four-patch*. This is made by dividing the basic block into four equal parts. This basic four-patch can be further subdivided to form variations like *Windmill Blades, Bow Tie* and *Dutchman's Puzzle*.

After the four-patch comes the *nine-patch* block. The basic nine-patch has the block divided into nine equal parts. These nine parts can then be further subdivided into a large number of variations. Figure 22 shows a few of the many traditional nine-patch blocks.

Many traditional block patterns are variations of the four-patch and nine-patch blocks. Others do not fall so readily into these simple groups. Amongst these are asymmetrical blocks and the many patterns based on plant and animal themes like *Spider Web, Flying Bats, Cactus Flower* and *Maple Leaf*.

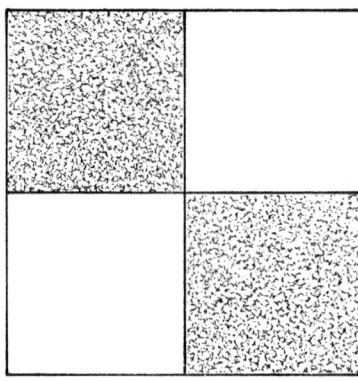

Basic four-patch

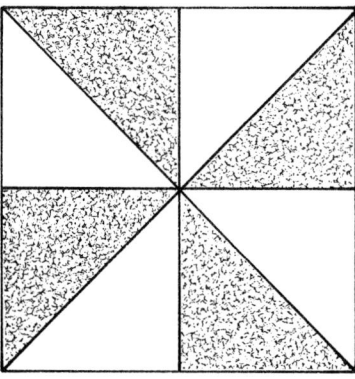

Windmill Blades

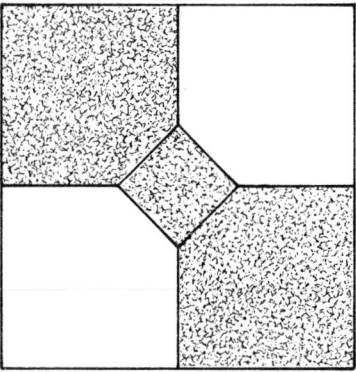

Bow Tie

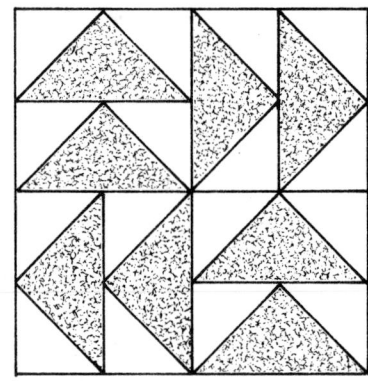

Dutchman's Puzzle

21 Basic four-patch and variations

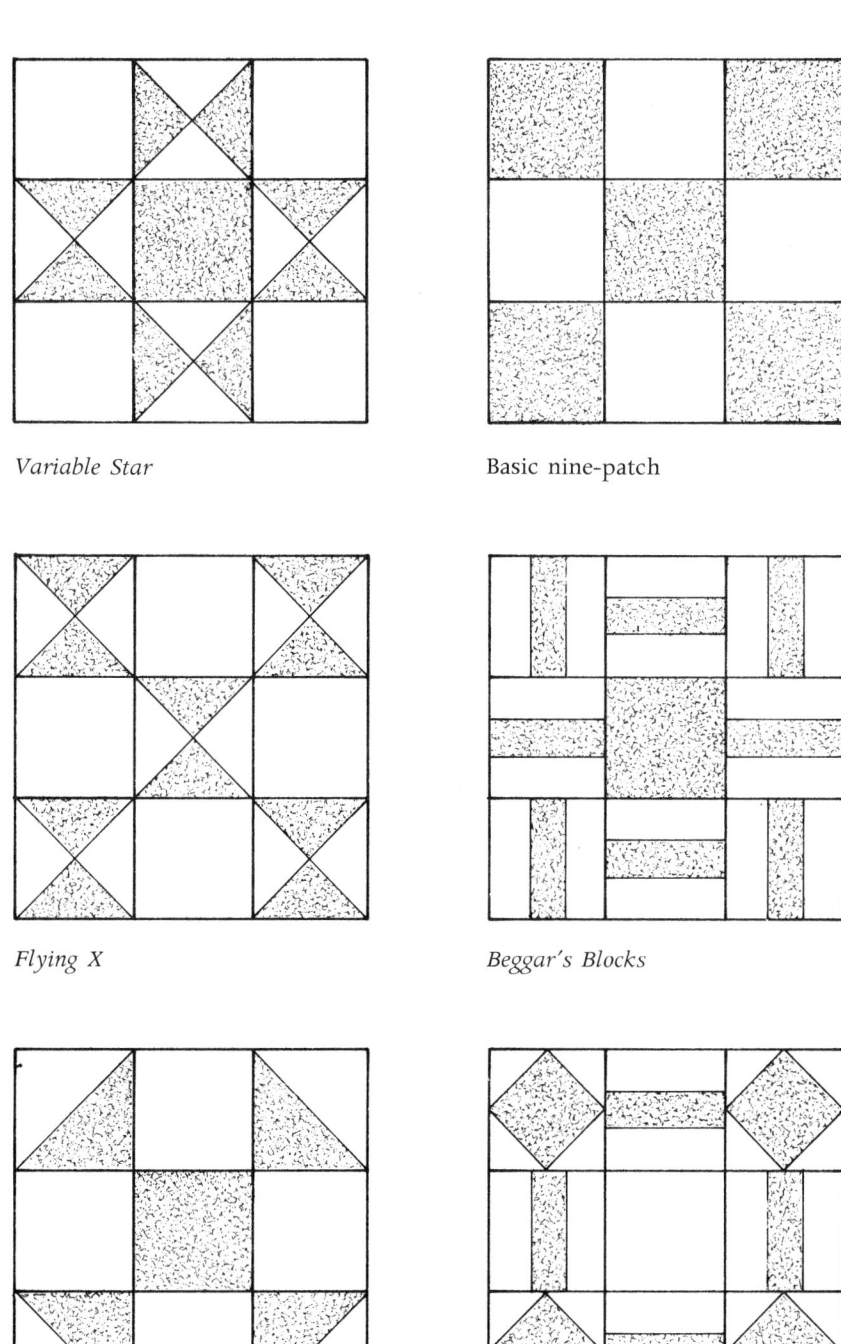

Variable Star

Basic nine-patch

Flying X

Beggar's Blocks

Shoo Fly

Kitty in the Corner

22   Basic nine-patch and
variations

Spider Web

Flying Bats

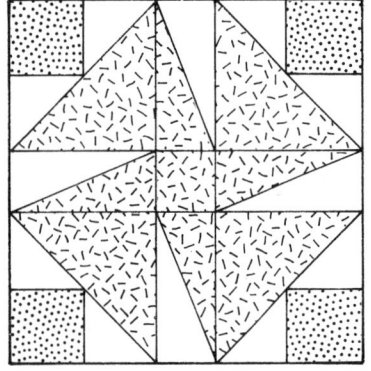

Follow-the-Leader

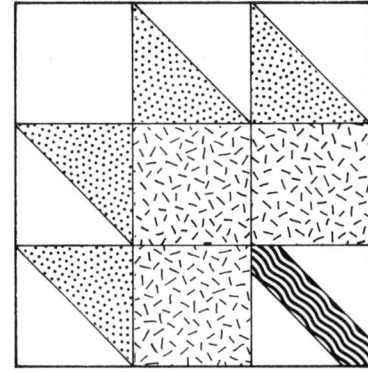

Maple Leaf

Cactus Basket

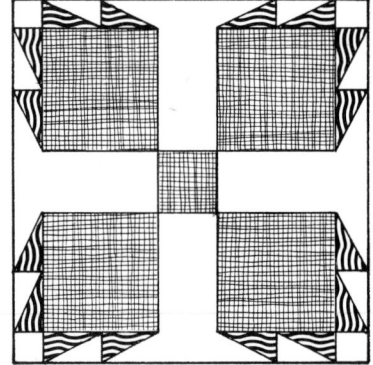

Bear's Paw

23 Selected block patterns

Setting blocks together

Setting is the term used to describe the manner in which blocks are joined one to another.

The simplest way to set blocks is to join them directly on the square, that is with the seams joining the blocks running horizontally and vertically. With blocks which have a four-fold symmetry, each block can be turned through 90° and the effect will be the same. If, however, your block pattern is asymmetrical or has a two-fold symmetry, you will find that different overall pattern effects can be created by turning the blocks around into different positions. The quilt illustrated in figure 31 is an excellent example of how the different orientation of each block combined with clever use of colour and fabric can produce a most attractive overall pattern. The basic block in this case is *Lady of the Lakes* – see if you can work it out!

Perhaps the best known examples of the pattern effects created by different arrangements of identical blocks are the variations of the basic *Log Cabin* pattern. If the basic *Log Cabin* block is made by combining light fabrics on one side of the diagonal and dark fabrics on the other, then the patterns known as *Straight Furrow, Diamonds* and *Barn Raising* will result merely by placing the *Log Cabin* squares in their appropriate positions. All these variations can also be worked with squares divided into dark and light triangles.

24 *Log Cabin* variations (bottom left block indicates how to piece each block)

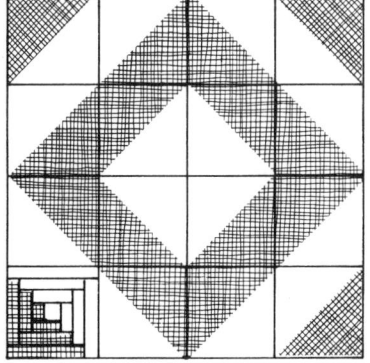

Barn Raising

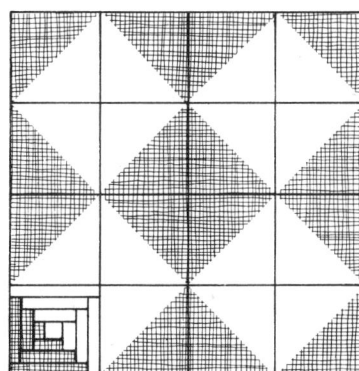

Diamonds

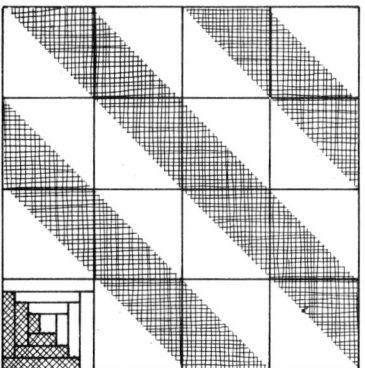

Straight Furrow

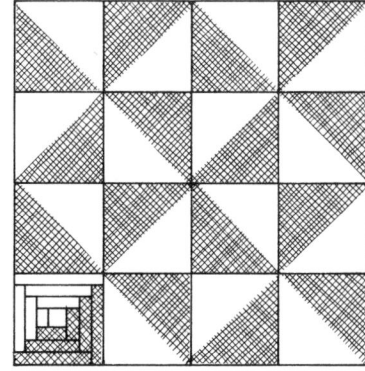

Windmill

43

Blocks can also be set on the diagonal, that is, with the seam joining the blocks running diagonally across the work. This can produce interesting variations on very simple designs. The quilts in figure 8 and colour plate facing page 72 show how blocks and even simpler squares can be set in this way. If this is done, however, triangular-shaped half blocks are needed to add at the edges if they are to be straight.

Sometimes blocks are set with fabric strips in between the blocks. These are known as *lattice strips* and the quilt in figure 4 illustrates their use.

Patchwork blocks of different patterns can be set together. Some traditional patterns like *Double Irish Chain* are a combination of two different blocks. Sometimes a combination of plain and patchwork blocks is used as in figure 10.

(a)   *Bars* – Amish style

26a–c   Selected overall patterns (reading across)

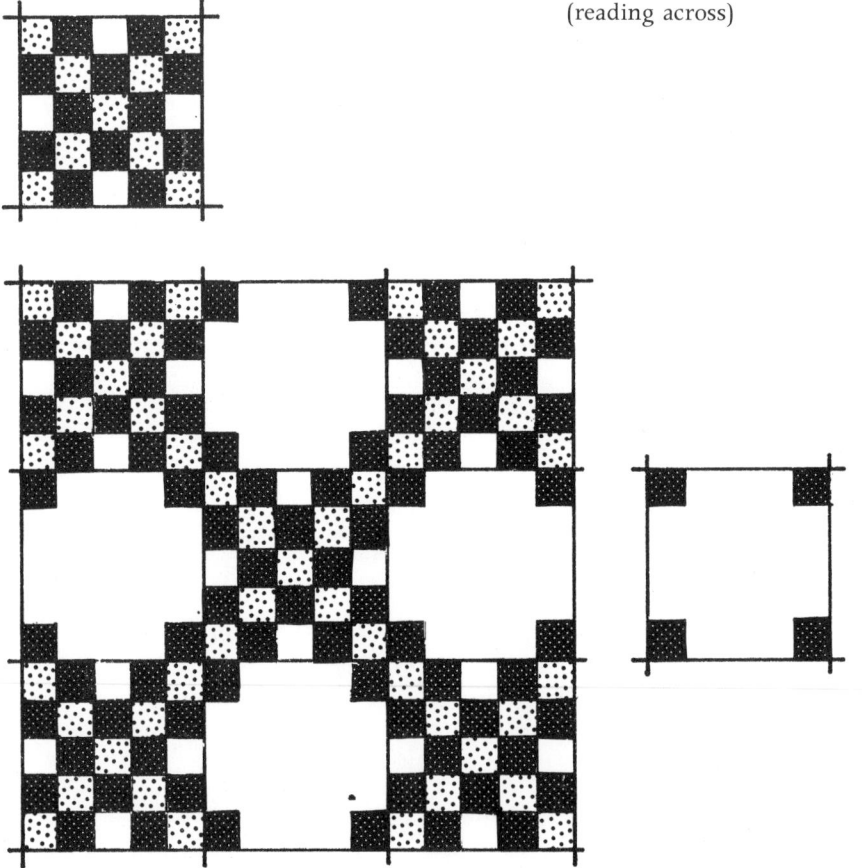

25   *Double Irish Chain* – a combination of two blocks

44

(b) *Lone Star* – Amish style

(c) 'Free' patchwork

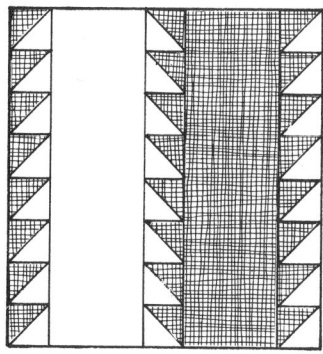

Tree Everlasting

Overall patterns

An overall pattern is a rather loose term to describe a pattern in which the whole patchwork is made up of units of different patterns, shapes and sizes. It includes the traditional medallion or framed patterns and also contemporary ideas like 'free patchwork' where the pattern is an abstract grouping of shapes and sizes. It also includes patterns like those of the Amish women, settlers in Pennsylvania of Dutch origin, who produced quilts of stunning design which have much in common with the bold work of some contemporary designers.

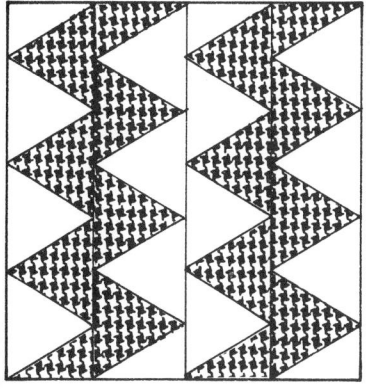

Streak o'Lightning
27 Two patterns pieced in strips

Strip patterns

Strip patterns include all those patterns where the basic shape in the patchwork is a fabric strip, like *Log Cabin, Courthouse Steps, Pineapple* and *Chevron*. Also included in this group are patterns like *Tree Everlasting* and *Lightning Strips* where the basic shapes are pieced into long strip units and these joined together to complete the patchwork.

Using colour in patchwork is very personal. Everyone has an individual attitude to colour – some people like bright colours, some like subdued colour, some like multi-coloured patchwork and others prefer a restricted use of colour. Particular colour combinations may be loved by some and hated by others. Choosing colours for patchwork is, in the end, a very intuitive and individual choice and you will learn by experience what works to your particular satisfaction.

It might help to consider a little colour theory. Every colour has three characteristics – hue, tone (or value) and intensity. The colour *hue* is the colour name – red, blue and yellow are primary hues and orange, green and purple (the colours produced when two of the primary colours are mixed) are secondary hues. These primary and secondary hues are combined to form the simple colour wheel below. If any of these six hues is combined with its neighbouring hue then the result is a tertiary hue, eg red-orange.

The *tone* of a colour is the light-value of the colour – how light or dark the hue is. This is an important characteristic of colour in patchwork because light colours will usually dominate in a pattern and dark colours recede. The relative position of the lights and darks in a pattern can make the same pattern appear quite different. Figure 30 illustrates this point. The same basic block pattern is shown with two different shadings. The overall pattern effect which results when a number of the blocks are combined is quite different in the two examples and is dominated by the light areas. You can spend an enjoyable hour or so playing about with different basic patterns and colouring them in alternate ways to see the effects created.

The *intensity* of a colour is the brightness or dullness of the hue. Bright colours will stand out and duller colours will recede so if you choose a bright red fabric it will stand out against a duller fabric of perhaps a lighter tone.

Any particular colour will also be affected by the other colours with which it is combined. When colours which are opposite on the colour wheel are combined, eg red and green, they intensify each other and can appear to vibrate. Colours which are close to each other on the colour wheel should blend harmoniously, though it is often true in patchwork that it is more difficult to successfully combine two or three fabrics than to combine twice that many.

All this colour theory is fine when you are using plain fabrics but it becomes more difficult to apply when using patterned ones. Patterned fabrics can range from two tones of one hue to multi-coloured fabrics in rainbow hues. How do you decide where a particular patterned fabric fits into the colour scheme? How is it going to look when you combine it with other fabrics? The only real answer to this is to learn by experience. However, you can try two things. First, you can squint at the fabric from a distance and see which colour appears to dominate and whether it appears as a light or dark fabric. In general, fabrics with the pattern on a light ground

Choosing colours

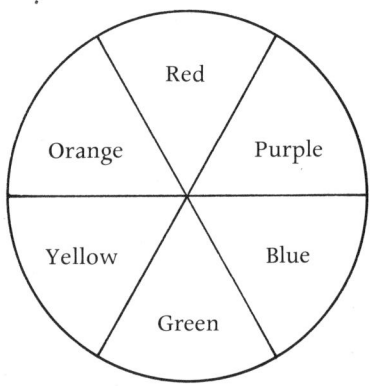

28   Colour wheel

will appear light in tone and the reverse will be true if the ground is dark. Secondly, you can try putting the fabric with the others you intend to combine in the patchwork and see how it reacts – does it stand out or does it recede in with the others. Choosing colours for patchwork cannot really be separated from choosing fabrics for the fabric is the medium you choose to represent the colour.

When choosing colours and fabrics for your patchwork, it is wise to consider the colours and other fabrics of the room which is intended as its 'home', if it is a domestic item. No matter how attractive the patchwork, it can be spoiled if it does not harmonize with the furnishings, colour and scale of the room.

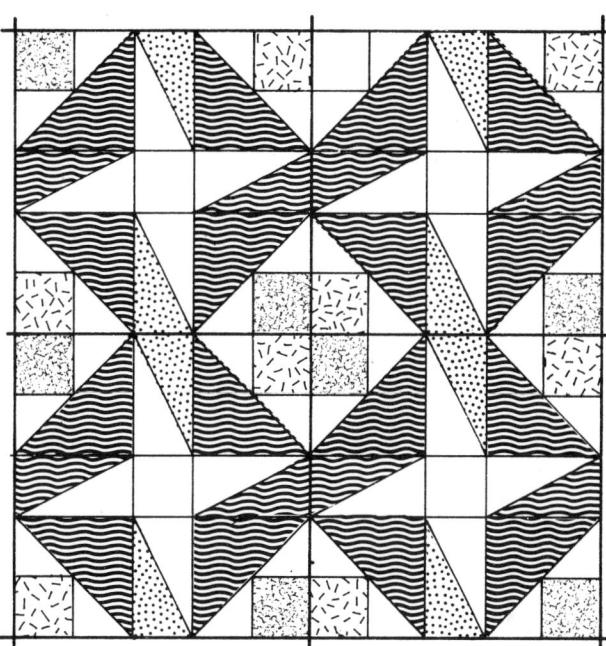

29 *Follow-the-Leader* in two different shadings

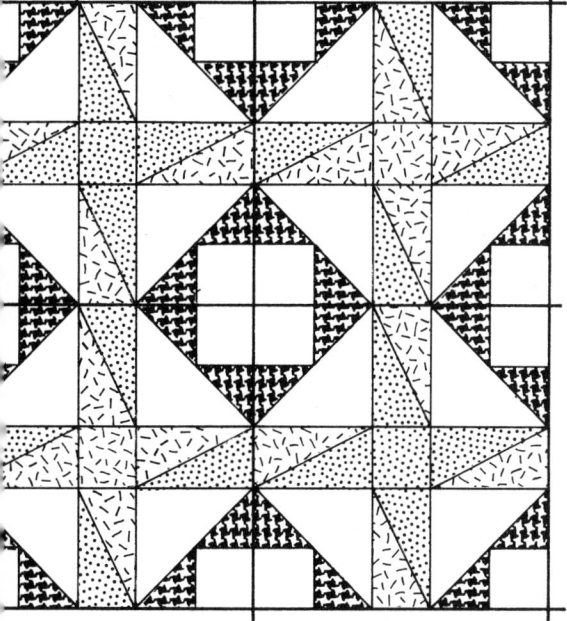

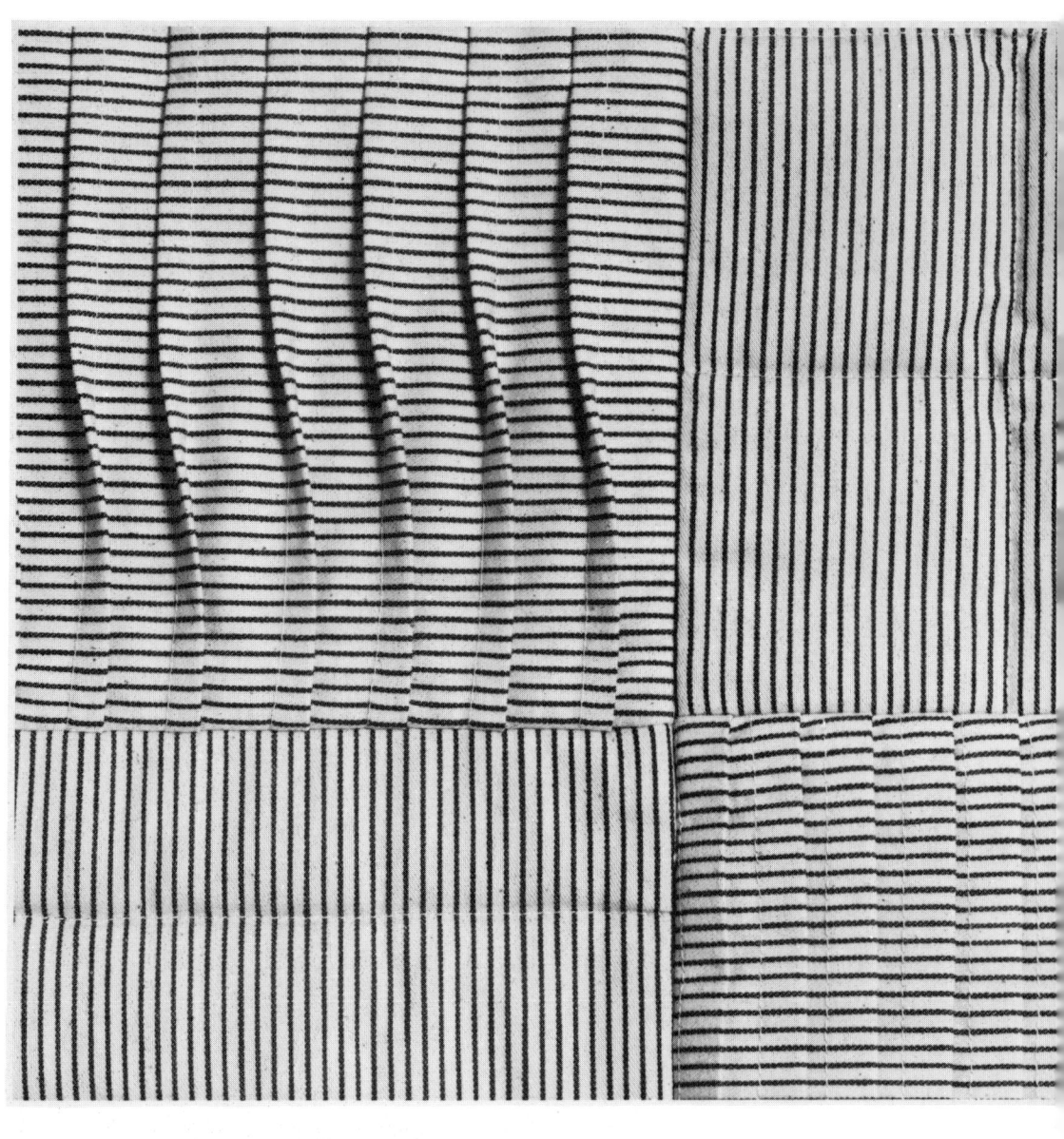

30   Detail of quilt by Eng Tow showing tucking, quilting and top-stitching

| Texture | Texture is the nature of the surface and, in patchwork, the texture of the fabrics used will affect the texture of the finished work accordingly. Using richly textured fabrics such as velvets, brocades and silks will bring a shiny, rich quality to the work whereas heavy woollen fabrics could look very tough and utilitarian. Combining fabrics of a similar texture usually works well but combining fabrics of different textures is more difficult to do successfully. It is always important to remember, however, not to piece fabrics of different weights directly together. |

Texture can be introduced to patchwork by using techniques like tucking, pleating, gathering and quilting. These techniques all add a new dimension – a relief – to patchwork and can enhance an otherwise flat piece of work.

Quilting has always been associated with patchwork not just for the added warmth a quilted layer will give but also the attractive texture it adds. Quilting adds softness and relief and when you have seen a piece of flat patchwork transformed by quilting, it is not difficult to understand why the two crafts are so closely associated.

Balance and proportion

Proportion means obtaining a pleasing relationship between the size of the patchwork shapes in relation to each other and to the overall work. Proportion also needs to be carefully considered when adding borders.

Balance means creating a balanced or stable look to your pattern. With a simple, repeated pattern, balance is not too difficult to achieve. It is more difficult with an overall design using a variety of shapes and sizes.

One of the reasons for making a scale diagram of your intended design, as will be described next, is to ensure that the balance and proportions are correct before you begin.

Drawing a scale diagram

Once you have decided on your pattern idea and colours, the texture you want to bring to your patchwork and the proportions, the next step is to draw out the design, to scale, on graph paper. Making a scale drawing in this way is a modern approach to patchwork but it is useful in many ways. At this stage you can experiment. You can take a traditional pattern and colour it in different ways, perhaps add a new shape or take one away to vary the basic pattern. Or if the pattern idea is your own concept, you can still draw it out, adjust it until the colours, the balance and proportions are right. Always make a complete drawing of the whole intended work – not just one block, for example – only then will you have a complete visual impression of the finished work. You will probably make not one drawing but several. But it is much quicker and cheaper to experiment on paper!

Choose a graph paper which is suitable for the pattern idea you have chosen. The paper with a triangular grid (Triangular Co-ordinate) can be used for patterns based on a hexagon, lozenge or half-lozenge shape but other patterns will require graph paper with a square grid. Graph paper can be obtained from a good stationers but if you have difficulty obtaining the Triangular Co-ordinate, try a students bookshop or artist's suppliers.

Choose a scale which is big enough to show up the elements of the pattern but convenient to work with. For example, if you were drawing out a nine-patch block on graph paper with a centimetre grid, you could use one centimetre square for each of the nine patches. If, however, you had graph paper with an inch grid, it would be impractical to use an inch square for each of the nine patches – if you were planning a large item the scale would be too large.

Once you have drawn out the pattern with pencil and ruler, colour it in several ways and then select out the scheme you prefer. You can use crayons, colouring pencils or felt-tip pens.

When you come to piecing your patchwork, keep the final drawing close at hand. You will find it an invaluable reference when working out which pieces fit next to each other.

Traditional patterns

Traditional patterns are those patterns which have been handed down through generations of patchworkers and whose originators are unknown. There are, literally, hundreds of known traditional patterns some dating back more than two centuries and others of more recent origin. Some are found on both sides of the Atlantic but many, especially the block patterns, are particularly North American. Some of the oldest patterns no doubt crossed the Atlantic with the early settlers to the New World but others evolved independently. It is very probable that similar or identical patterns evolved independently in different parts of North America since many block patterns are simple variations on a common theme.

The names given to traditional patterns are almost entirely North American in origin and many have already been referred to. It is beyond the scope of this book to consider in any detail the origin and history of pattern names but if the reader is interested, I suggest they read the relevant sections in Ruth E. Finley's book *Old Patchwork Quilts*.

Contemporary patchwork

Perhaps the most encouraging aspect of the current revival of interest in patchwork is the excellent contemporary work being done on both sides of the Atlantic. This new and original work represents not just a revival but a revitalisation of the craft. And with this revitalisation has come a new attitude. Patchwork and quilting are not just domestic crafts but crafts in which the standard of artistic achievement is every bit as high as in other art media. Patchwork is finding its way out of the home and into art galleries and museums.

Many contemporary workers still work within the broad framework of traditional style and pattern either by interpreting

31 Quilt *Lady of the Lakes* by Barbara Robson, Nova Scotia

32   Quilt *Crow's Nest* by Barbara Robson

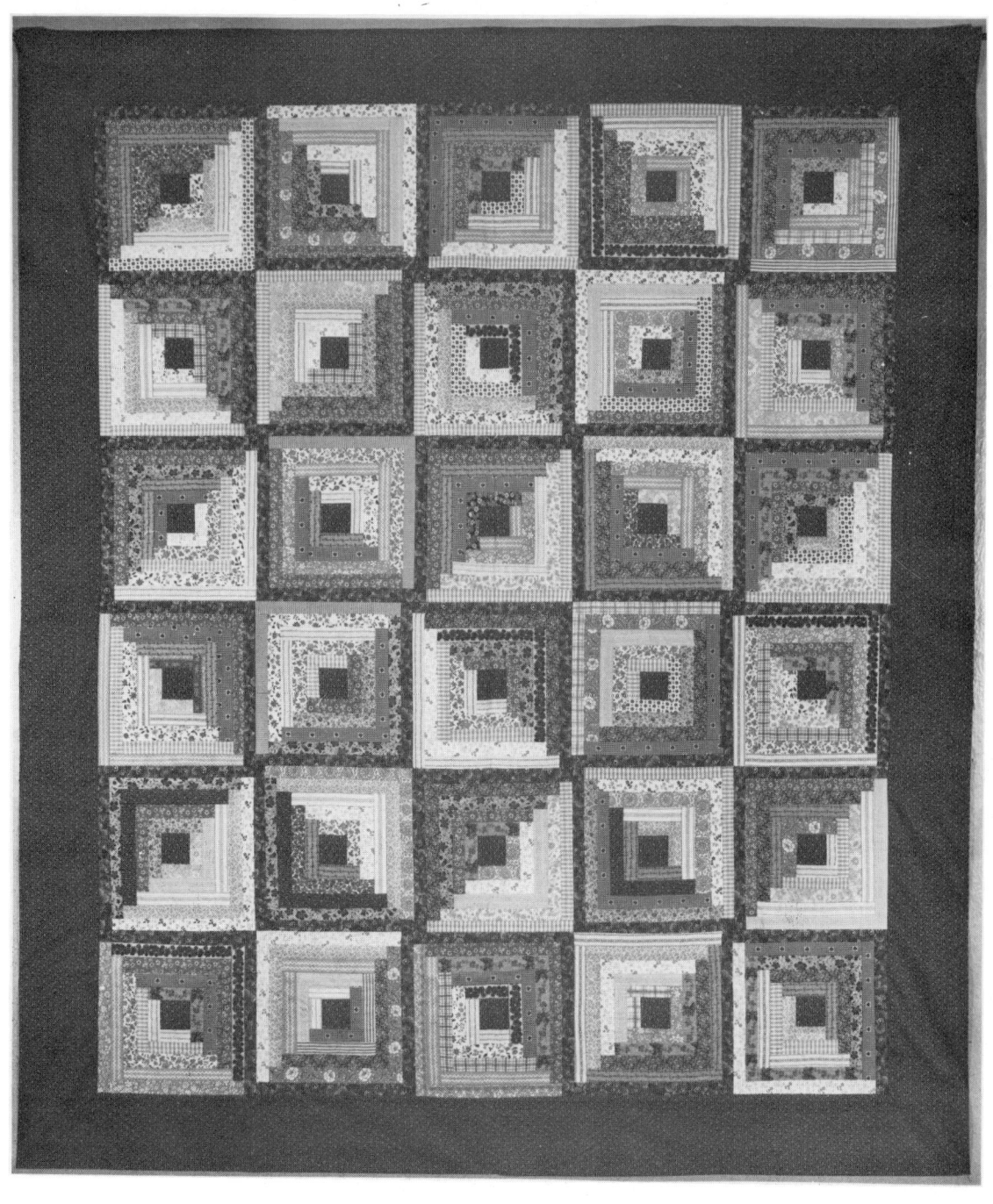

33 Bedspread pieced in the *Windmill* variation of *Log Cabin* by
Janet Jacobson, Northumberland

and adapting well-known patterns or creating original patterns and piecing them in the traditional style. Other designers have broken away completely from the traditional framework to create wholly original designs.

It is hard to categorise contemporary patchwork because so many new avenues are being explored. Much is bold in style and vivid in colour. Quilting is frequently used with patchwork and this, too, is often bold in line in contrast to the elaborate, flowing patterns of traditional quilting. There is much good, innovative design with designers tending to explore and develop their own particular themes so their work has that individual 'stamp'.

New tools and materials have influenced contemporary patchwork. The sewing machine is widely used both for patchwork and quilting. The relative speed with which piecing can be done by machine has made it possible for some designers to seek a living from their craft. Some might regard the commercialisation of the craft as a retrograde step but if it results in good new ideas and healthy competition for well-made and well-designed work, then I feel it can only represent a step forward.

The arrival of polyester wadding has also had some influence on contemporary styles. Because it can be easily worked on the machine, it is possible to sew patches directly on the wadding using it as foundation cloth. This opens up enormous possibilities just a few of which will be illustrated in this book. Polyester wadding also holds together firmly in washing so, if the patchwork is quilted, the quilting lines do not need to be as close as in traditional work.

The work illustrated in figures 31–41 is a small selection of the excellent patchwork and quilting produced by contemporary designers and shows something of the range of work being done. The quilts by Barbara Robson and Janet Jacobson are excellent examples of how individual feel for colour and fabric can be used to interpret time-honoured patterns. The bold, geometric and colourful pieces of Dierdre Amsden are in sharp contrast to the restrained work of Eng Tow which shows such original and precise use of tucks and pleats to give texture and relief. In another direction, Pauline Burbidge's quilts show her clever use of shapes to create patchwork with a strong representational content.

This contemporary work is, of course, the result of experience and experiment. But anyone can create their own original design ideas, or interpret traditional patterns in their own way, once they have understood and mastered the simple techniques of patchwork.

34   Bedspread pieced in a one-patch pattern of triangles by Janet
Jacobson

35 Quilted wall hanging by Dierdre Amsden, Cambridge

36 Quilted wall hanging by Dierdre Amsden

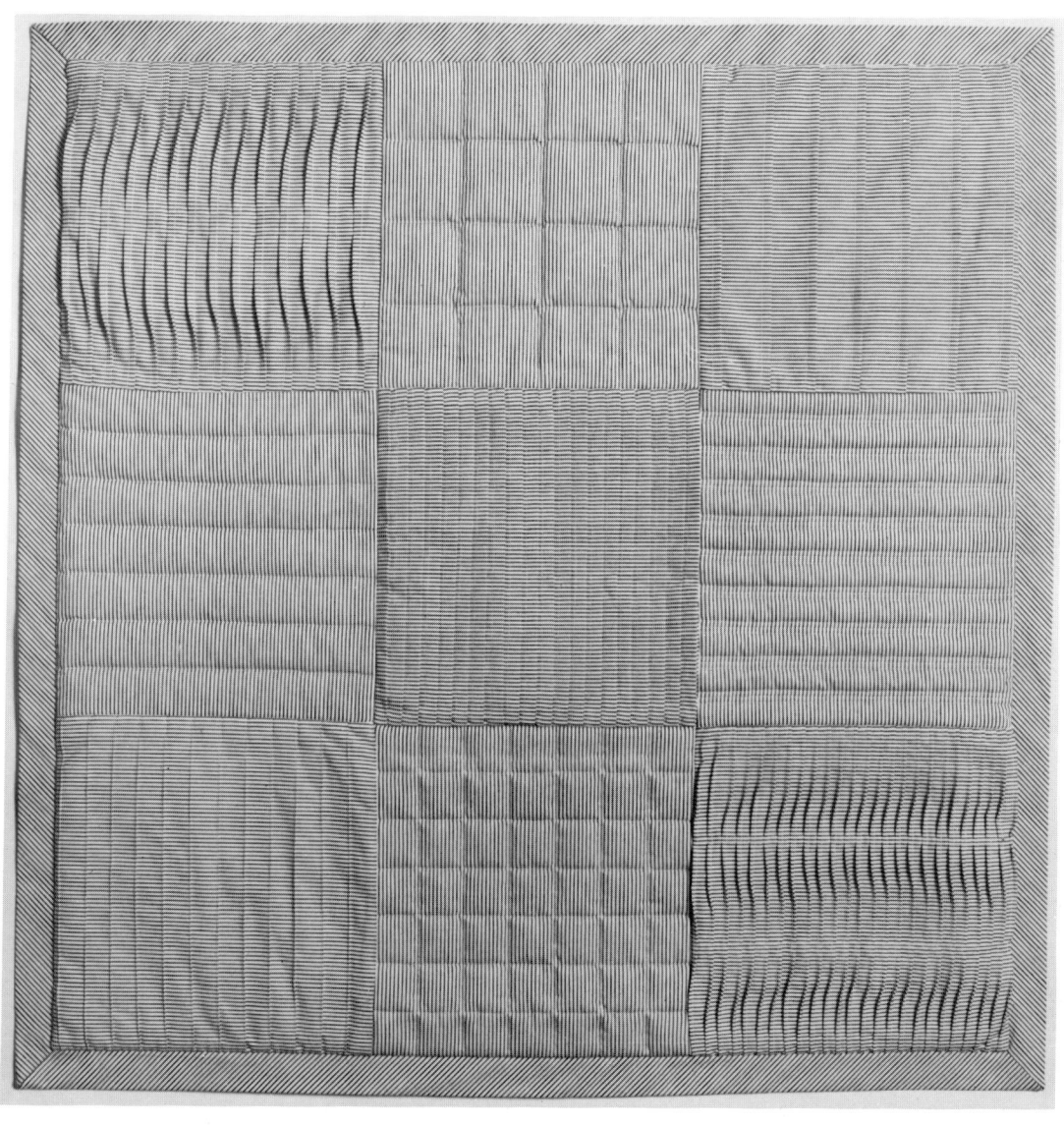

37 Quilt in cotton ticking by Eng Tow, London and Singapore

38   Tucked and quilted cushions in white by Eng Tow

39   Quilt *Korky the Cat* by Pauline Burbidge, London, in 3.8 cm (1½ in) cotton squares

40   Quilt *Landscape Garden* by Pauline Burbidge in hand-dyed cotton

41   Quilted wall hanging *Fruit Basket* by Pauline Burbidge in hand-dyed cotton

Making templates and marking foundation cloth

Good patchwork must be accurate and the only way to achieve this accuracy is to ensure that each piece of fabric in the pattern is exactly the size it ought to be.

There are two ways this can be done. First, you can make a template for each *different shape* used in the pattern. This template is then used to draw the shape onto the fabric before it is cut out. This method is used when piecing geometrical shapes directly together. You do not need a paper template for each individual patch as is the case when hand-sewing in the traditional 'English' manner.

The second method is used for any pattern where the fabric strips or pieces are sewn onto foundation cloth. In this case, the foundation cloth is marked with clear, accurate guidelines to ensure that each piece is sewn in its correct position.

Making templates

The templates I use when piecing patchwork by machine are made to the exact size of the patch as it will appear in the finished work. The seam allowance is *not* included. The reason for this is that when the shape is drawn around the template onto the fabric, the line produced gives a clear, accurate guideline for machining along when piecing. When the patches are cut out, *then* the appropriate seam allowance is left around the outline shapes.

You can, of course, buy templates. Most needlecraft shops and haberdashery departments now stock a variety of templates, usually of metal or plastic. These are tough materials and will therefore last a long time and, for that reason, may be worth investing in. However, you will be limited to the sizes and shapes available in the stores.

Making your own templates is not difficult and much cheaper. The women who made patchwork quilts in the good old days certainly never bought their templates. They made their own from card or stiff paper and, if necessary, got their men-folk to make them wooden ones (you could try that too!).

Most home-made templates are made from card or medium-grade sandpaper but you can, if you want them to last longer, make them of sheet metal or perspex. Sandpaper may seem an unlikely material to use but it does have the advantage that, when the template is used sand-side down, the fabric is gripped firmly by the texture of the paper and does not slip as you draw around it. I use sandpaper templates for this reason. The disadvantage with sandpaper and card is that the corners wear away quickly and you will need to make several templates of the same shape if you are making a big item. Ideally, you could glue the sandpaper to metal or wood to get the best of both worlds. If you use thin model-makers' plywood, this can be cut with scissors.

The basic method for making templates is the same for any shape and can be summed up in the following stages:

1   Using a ruler and pencil, draw your shape accurately, full-size,

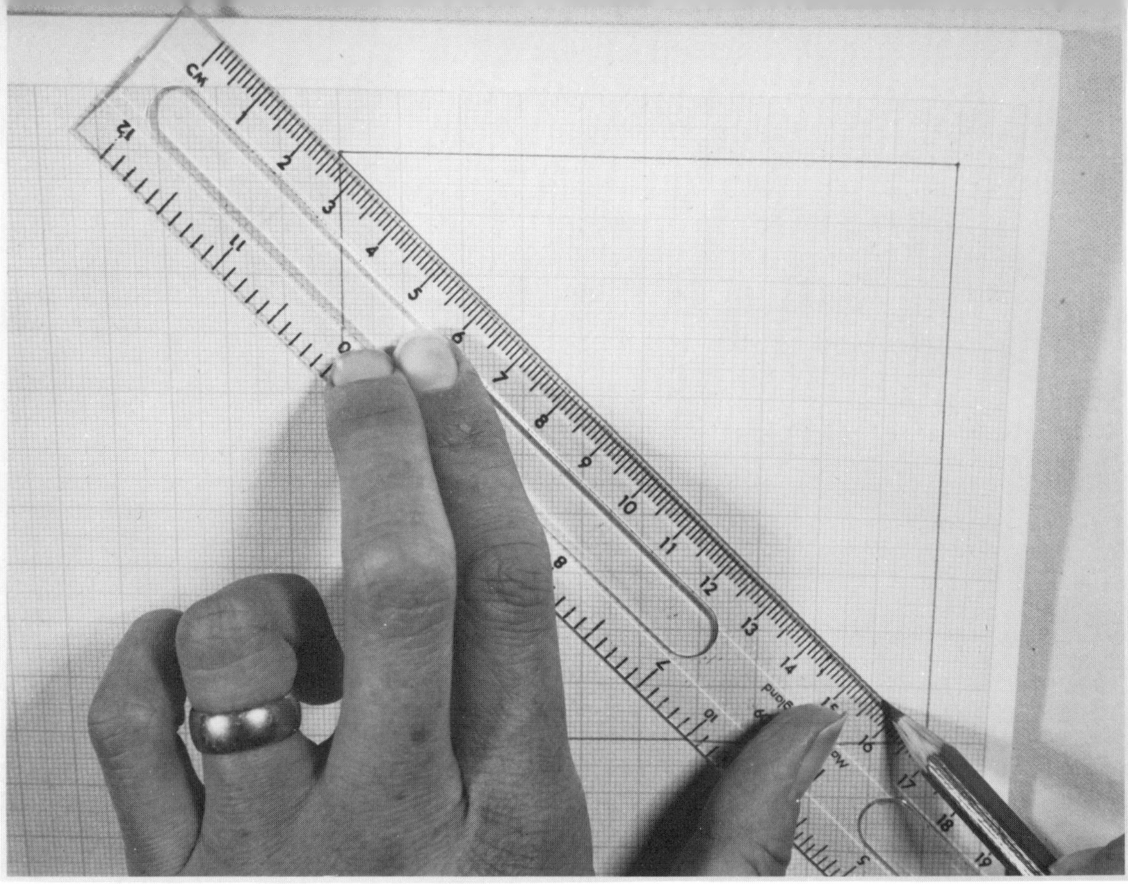

42 Stages in making templates

(a) Stage 1

(b) Stage 2

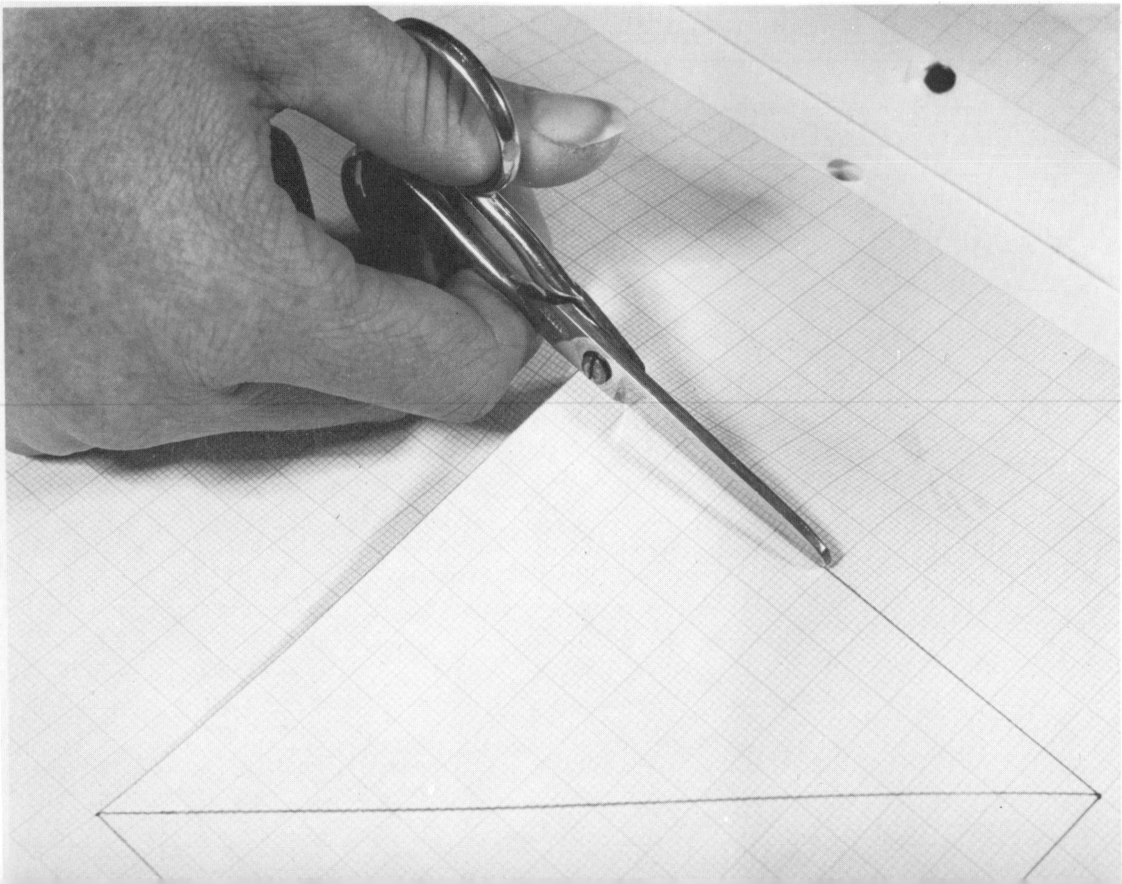

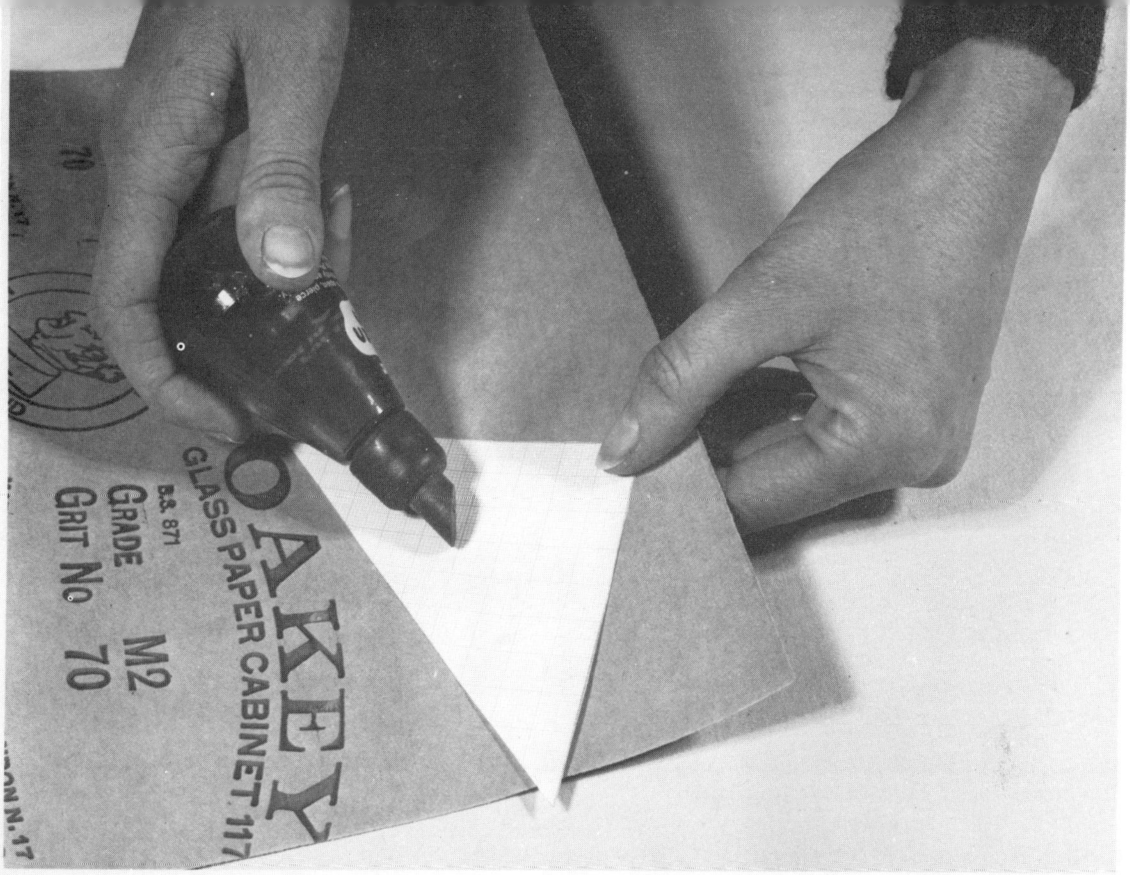

(c) Stage 3

(d) Stage 4

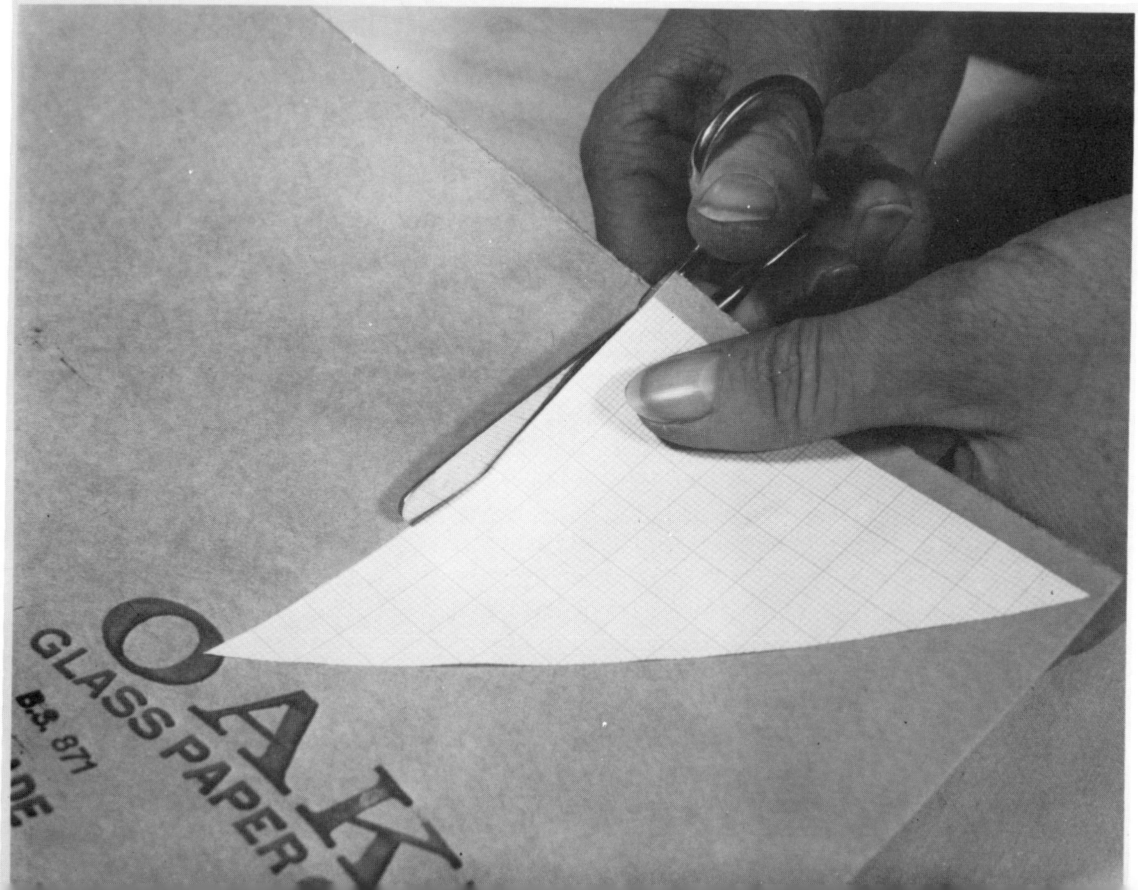

on graph paper. Pencils must always be kept well sharpened for drawing out shapes. (Figure 42a)

2   Cut out the shape. (Figure 42b)

3   Glue the cut-out shape onto stiff card or sandpaper. If you want the shape to last use perspex, sheet-metal or plywood. (Figure 42c)

4   Cut out carefully around the glued shape. Scissors can be used to cut around sandpaper and thin plywood (*not* your best fabric scissors). Stiff card will need a rule and sharp craft-knife, perspex will need a hacksaw and sheet-metal will need metal shears. Your template is now ready to use. (Figure 42d)

The first stage is the critical one because you must ensure that the initial shape is accurate. All the angles and lengths of the sides in the shape must be correct otherwise your patchwork will not fit together properly.

The simplest way to achieve this accuracy is to draw your shape out, full size, on graph paper and this is the method I shall describe where possible. Using the appropriate graph paper (see page 22) most of the common geometrical shapes used in patchwork can be drawn.

All these shapes can also be constructed geometrically using a protractor and a pair of compasses. This type of construction is described in most elementary books of geometry. I have not described this method in detail except where it is the only accurate method available.

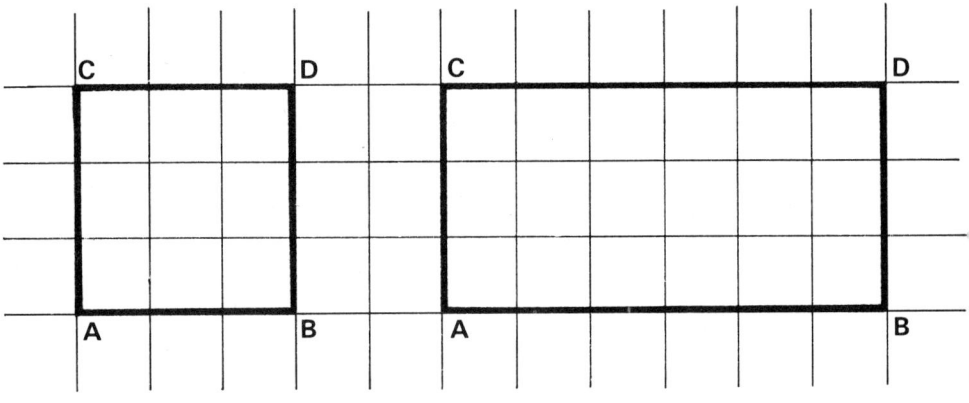

43   Drawing a square and a rectangle

Squares and rectangles

1   Using graph paper with a square grid, draw horizontal line AB the length of one side of your chosen square or rectangle.

2   From point A and point B, draw lines AC and BD perpendicular to AB by following or drawing parallel to a grid line. AC and BD should be the required length of the chosen square or rectangle.

3   Join CD to complete the shape.

4   Cut out, mount and complete the template.

Diamonds

Two diamond shapes are commonly used in patchwork – the long-diamond and the lozenge (wide-diamond). The long diamond has an angle of 45° in the apex and the lozenge an angle of 60°. Thus, eight long-diamonds put together will form an eight-pointed star and six lozenges will form a six-pointed star. Three lozenge shapes together form a hexagon – this is the basis of the Baby Blocks pattern.

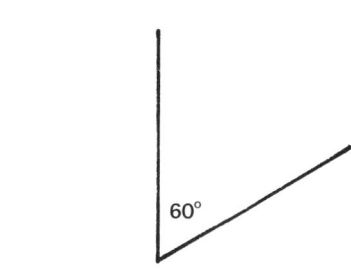

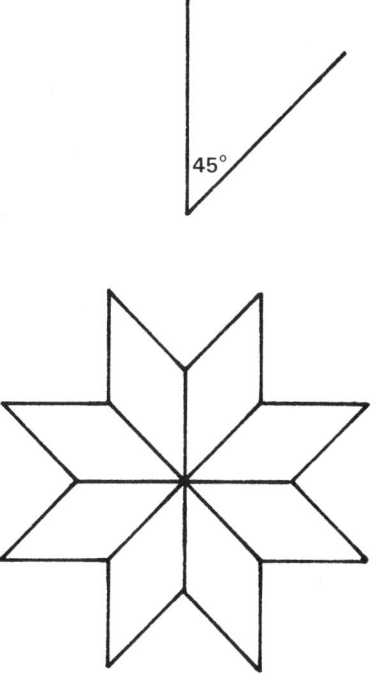

Eight-pointed star

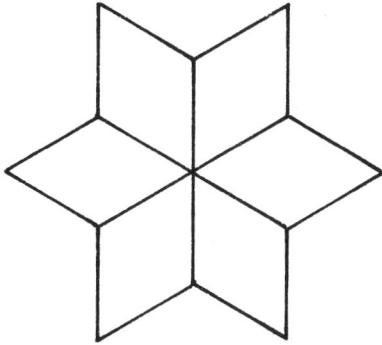

Six-pointed star

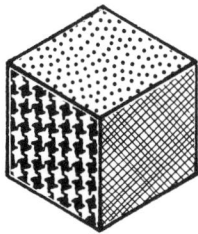

Baby blocks (three lozenges)

44   Diamonds

65

Lozenge (wide-diamond)

1   Using Triangular Co-ordinate graph paper, draw line AB the length of the side of the chosen diamond along the grid line running at 2 o'clock from any point on the grid (see figure 45).

2   From point A, draw line AD along the next grid line in a clockwise direction. The length AD equals AB.

3   From point B, draw line BC along the fourth grid line in a clockwise direction. The length BC equals AC and AD.

4   Join CD to complete the shape.

5   Cut out, mount and complete the template.

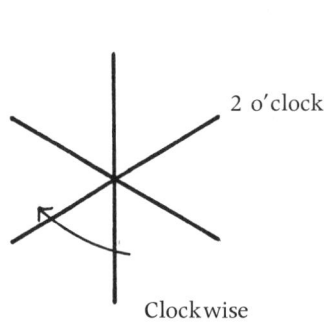

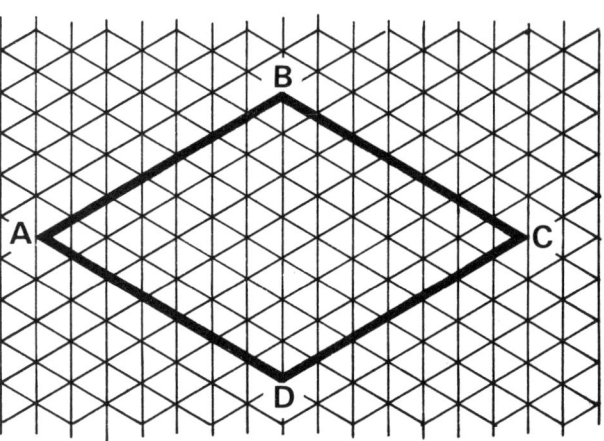

45   Drawing a lozenge

Long-diamond

This shape cannot be drawn accurately without the use of a protractor or 45° set-square and pair of compasses. Plain paper is therefore most suitable.

1   Using a ruler and pencil, draw a line AB the length of the side of the chosen diamond.

2   At point A use a protractor or 45° set-square to draw a line AC at 45° from AB. Mark off AC to equal AB.

3   Take the pair of compasses and set them at the length AB. With the compass point on C, make an arc in the area of D. With the compass point on B, make an arc of the same radius to cut the first arc. The point D is where the two arcs cross.

4   Join BD and CD to complete the shape.

5   Cut out, mount and complete the template.

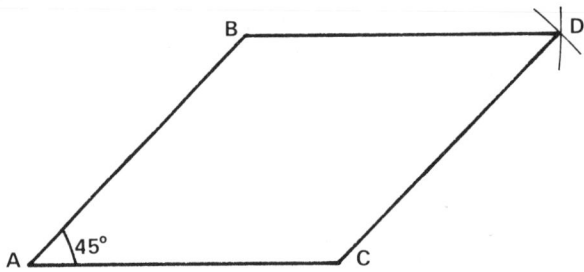

46   Constructing a long diamond

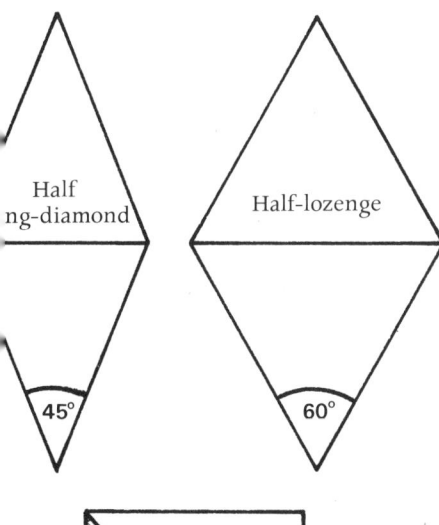

Half
ng-diamond   Half-lozenge

45°   60°

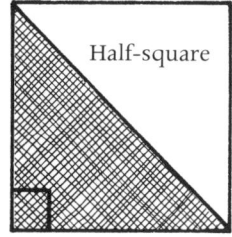

Half-square

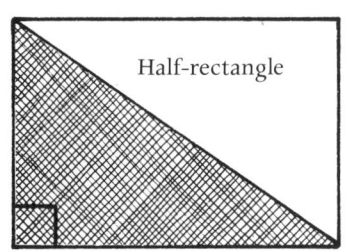

Half-rectangle

47 Triangles

Triangles
The four triangles illustrated in figure 47 are commonly used in patchwork. Instructions have already been given for the full shapes – squares, rectangles and diamonds – so for the corresponding triangle, draw out the full shape and divide in half. Cut out, mount and complete the templates.

Hexagons
1 Using Triangular Co-ordinate graph paper, draw line AB, the length of the chosen hexagon along one of the grid lines.
2 At point B, counting in a clockwise direction, draw the line BC on or parallel to the fourth grid line round from the line AB. This should give an angle of 120° between AB and AC and AB should equal BC.
3 At point C, repeat as for point B and draw line CD. CD equals AB.
4 At point D, repeat as for point B and draw line DE. DE equals AB.
5 At point E, repeat as for point B and draw line EF. EF equals AB.
6 Joint AF to complete shape.
7 Cut out, mount and complete the template.

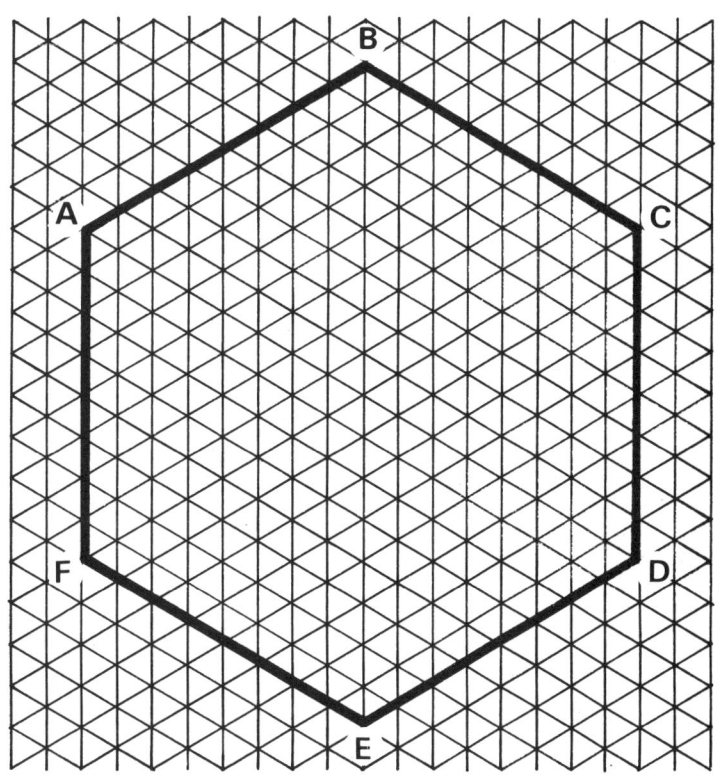

48 Drawing a hexagon

Block patterns

If you are using a block pattern which combines several different shapes, it may be simpler to draw out the complete block, full size, on paper. Graph paper will help to keep the shapes accurate. Cut out the individual shapes and use one of each different shape to complete the templates.

Marking out foundation cloth is a relatively simple process. Effectively, you need to draw out the required pattern on the foundation cloth using a ruler and sharp, but soft, pencil. This will give a series of guidelines indicating the exact position for each piece of fabric in the patchwork.

The most suitable fabric to buy for foundation cloth is cotton calico but be sure to wash it well first. If you buy unbleached calico, wash it at least twice to pre-shrink it and remove the colour. You can, of course, use old white cotton sheets (not too worn), curtain lining or similar fabrics you may have at home.

The following two examples will illustrate how to proceed with marking foundation cloth.

Log Cabin block

The cushion illustrated in figure 50 is made of four *Log Cabin* blocks combined in the *Diamond* pattern. Each block has a centre of 2.5 cm (1 in) and five rows of strips around the centre with each strip 2 cm ($\frac{3}{4}$ in) wide. The size of the completed block is 21.5 cm ($8\frac{1}{2}$ in). Each block was marked out in the following way and illustrated in figure 49.

1   Cut foundation fabric to the size of the completed block plus 2 cm ($\frac{3}{4}$ in) all round for seam allowance. Follow the lines of the fabric weave to ensure that the block is square
2   Draw diagonal lines from corner to corner. The centre of the block is where the two lines cross
3   From centre, measure outwards 12 mm ($\frac{1}{2}$ in) on all four sides and draw in centre square following fabric weave
4   On all four sides of the centre square mark five divisions of 2 cm ($\frac{3}{4}$ in) from centre square outwards
5   Draw lines, parallel to sides of the centre square, running through these divisions and extending about 12 mm ($\frac{1}{2}$ in) beyond the diagonal lines. This slight extension of the line will prove very useful when you sew

The square block is now ready for the patchwork. Any *Log Cabin* or *Courthouse Steps* block can be marked in this manner using whatever dimensions are required. *Log Cabin* blocks can be made to any size and any width of strip can be used.

50   *Log Cabin* cushion

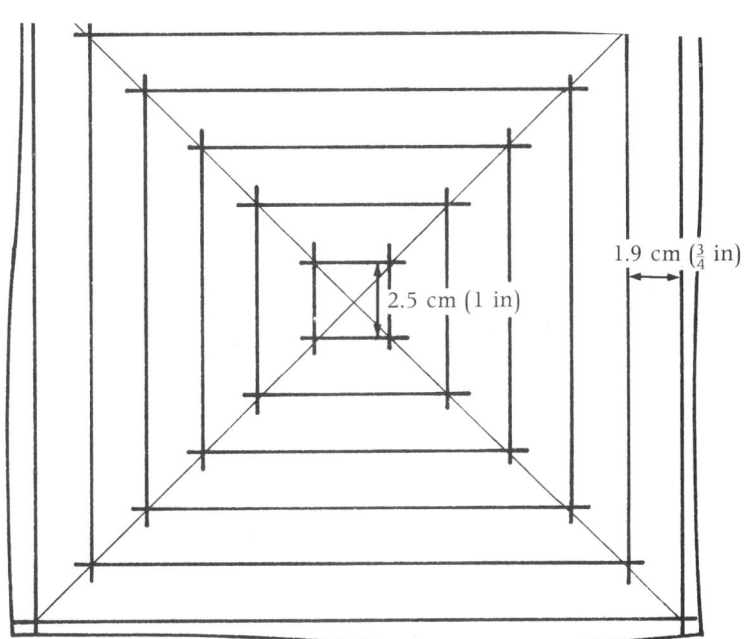

1.9 cm ($\frac{3}{4}$ in)

2.5 cm (1 in)

49   Marking foundation cloth for
Log Cabin block

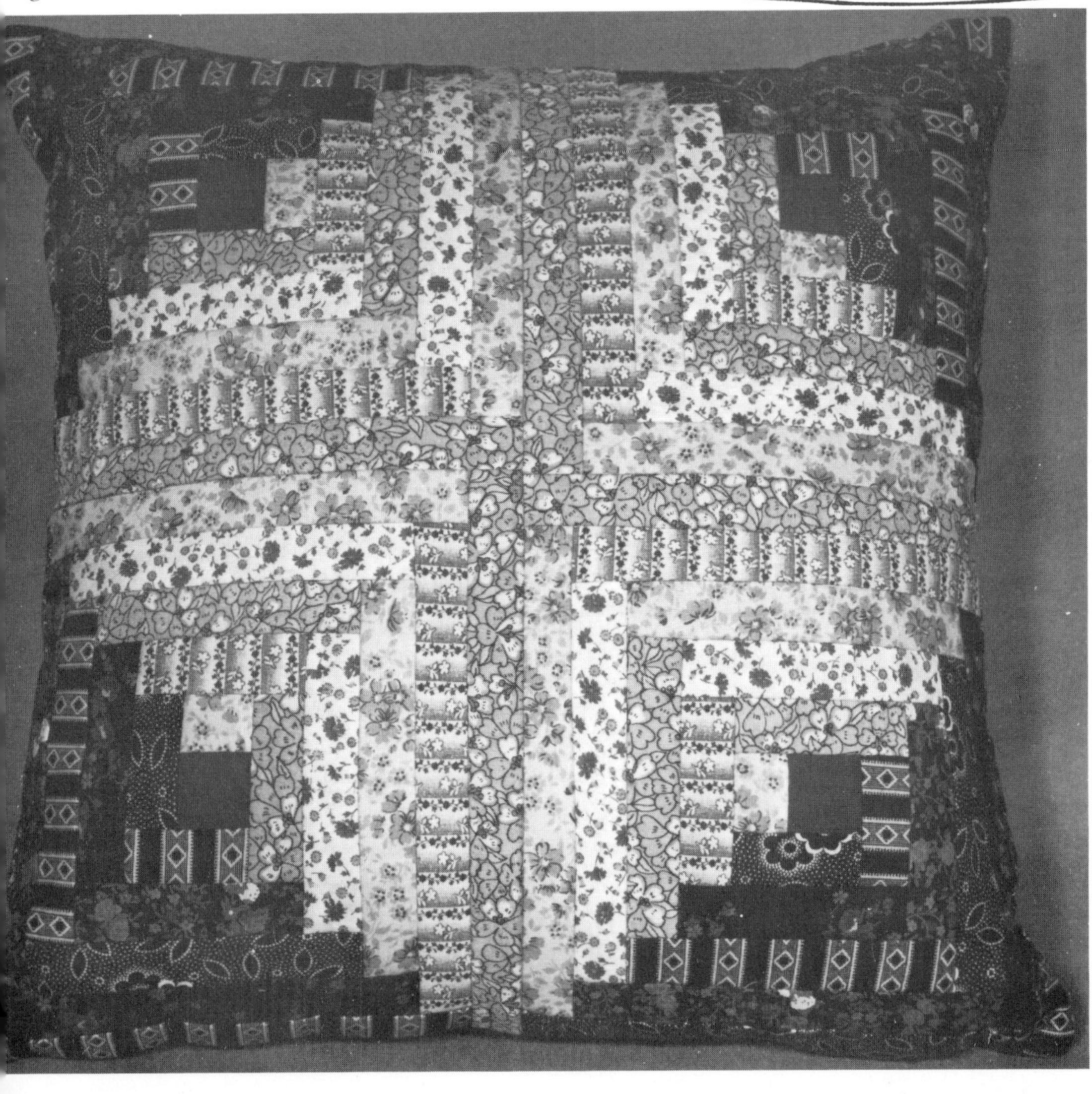

Chevron pattern

The cushion illustrated in figure 52 is made by sewing patchwork strips onto lengths of foundation cloth and joining the lengths together to complete the patchwork. The completed dimensions for each length and the patchwork strips used are given in figure 51 and the foundation cloth is marked in the following way:

1   Cut foundation fabric lengths to the size of the completed lengths plus 12 mm ($\frac{1}{2}$ in) all round for seam allowance.

2   On all four sides mark inwards 12 mm ($\frac{1}{2}$ in) and draw lines to represent seam line for joining lengths and completing cushion.

3   Mark eight divisions each of 3.8 cm ($1\frac{1}{2}$ in) along the two long edges.

4   Draw diagonal lines joining up the divisions as in figure 51. Join three lengths in this manner and reverse lines on the other two so that the *Chevron* pattern is formed when the lengths are joined in the correct order.

NOTE   a sequence of ten strips is required using these particular dimensions.

The lengths are now ready for the patchwork. Any *Chevron* pattern can be marked out in this manner to the required dimensions.

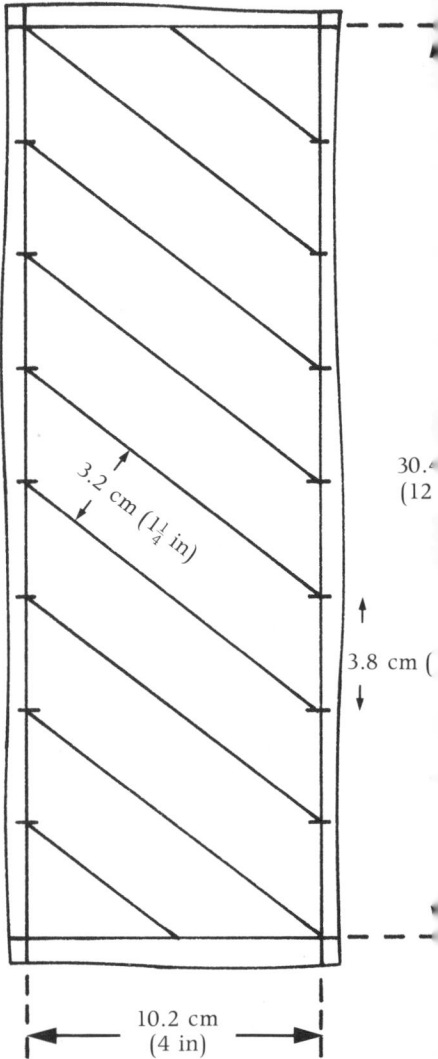

3.2 cm ($1\frac{1}{4}$ in)

30.4
(12

3.8 cm (

10.2 cm
(4 in)

51   Marking out a *Chevron* strip

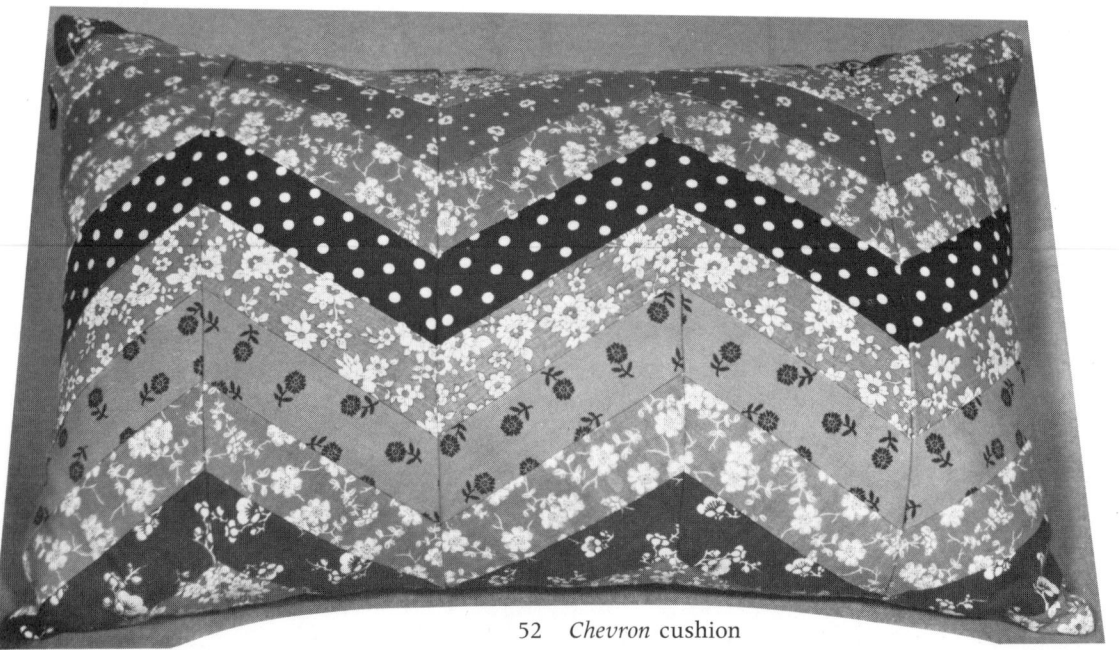

52   *Chevron* cushion

Cutting Out

Geometrical shapes

When geometrical shapes are pieced directly together, each piece of each shape must be cut individually. The templates are used to mark the shape accurately onto the fabric and after the shapes are marked out, the individual pieces are cut out.

Before cutting out any fabric pieces for your patchwork you should work out from your design how many patches of each shape you require and how many shapes need to be cut from each of the chosen fabrics. Take, for example, the *Jacob's Ladder* block illustrated in figure 53. This requires twenty small squares and eight triangles. From the shading you can see that ten squares are cut from one fabric, the other ten squares and four triangles are cut from a second fabric and the remaining four triangles are cut from a third fabric.

Before starting to mark out any shapes, all fabrics should be carefully pressed to remove any creases. This is an important step so do not be tempted to skip it – it is much more difficult to remove creases from the finished patchwork. It is also much easier to piece together well-ironed patches.

When the templates are laid down on the fabric, care should be taken to orientate the same shapes in the same way on the fabric. Squares and rectangles should always have their sides parallel to the fabric weave to avoid bias seams. Other shapes cannot avoid having some bias seams but these should be as few as possible. Figure 54 gives the suggested orientation to use for common geometrical shapes where possible.

Take care with the position of templates in relation to the fabric pattern. If the pattern is a small random one this position will not matter too much. But if you are using a large scale pattern or a fabric with stripes or checks or any linear pattern, then you need to position templates carefully to ensure the fabric is cut in the way you want it to appear in the patchwork. Sometimes window templates (templates with the centres cut away) or transparent templates are used for this purpose. Avoid including selvedge edges in your patchwork pieces because the perforated edges may show in your finished work.

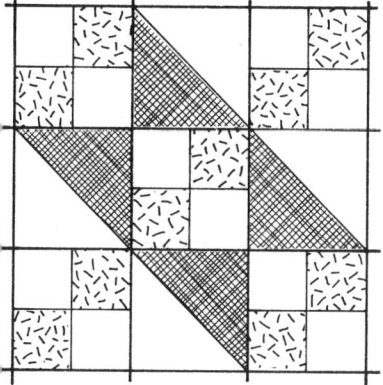

53   *Jacob's Ladder* block

54   Suggested orientation for cutting out common geometrical shapes

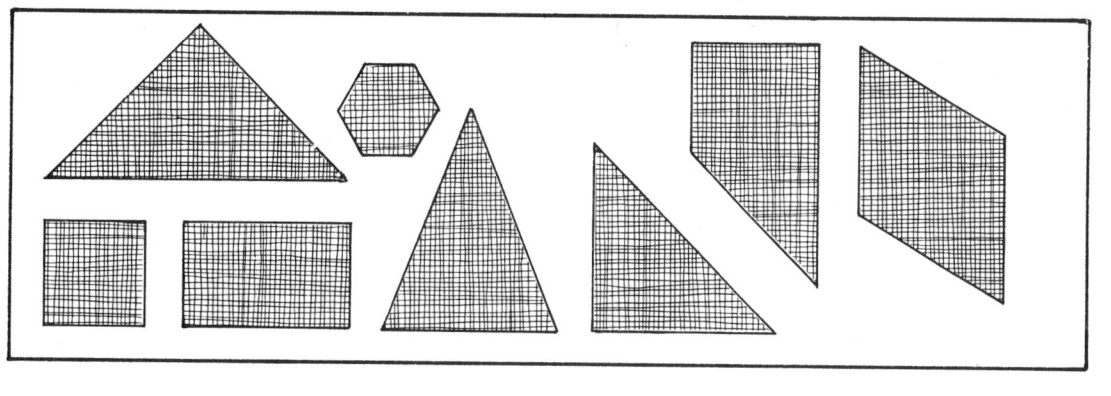

Fabric weave

71

Be especially careful with any asymmetrical shapes such as trapezoids. When laying the template on the wrong side of the fabric, be sure it is the opposite way round to the shape as it will appear in the finished work (see figure 55). If you cut these shapes out incorrectly they will not fit – it is like taking a dress-making pattern and cutting out two right fronts instead of a right and left. When making templates for these asymmetrical shapes which have a specific topside and underside, like sandpaper templates, be sure you have made the templates the correct way round.

When you cut out the shape, you will need to leave the appropriate seam allowance all around the marked shape. In most cases a seam allowance of 1 cm ($\frac{3}{8}$ in) will be adequate but with very small patches this may give too much bulk in the seams in relation to the size of the patch. In these cases the seam allowance could be cut to 6 mm ($\frac{1}{4}$ in).

The stages in marking and cutting out geometrical shapes can be summed up as follows:

1 Decide the orientation and positioning of your templates. Lay the template on the wrong side of the fabric.

2 Holding the template firmly, draw all round the edges onto the fabric with a soft, sharp pencil. On dark fabrics use a white chalk pencil. (Figure 56a).

3 Cut out the shape using sharp fabric scissors leaving the appropriate seam allowance all round. (Figure 56b).

Log Cabin and other patterns using patchwork strips do not require every individual piece to be cut separately before piecing provided they are being sewn onto a foundation cloth. The strips can be cut to an appropriate length after they have been sewn. The fabric only requires cutting or tearing into strips of the appropriate width, ie the width of the finished strip in the patchwork plus 6 mm ($\frac{1}{4}$ in) seam allowance on either side. So if the finished strips are to be 2.5 cm (1 in) wide, the strips need to be cut 4 cm ($1\frac{1}{2}$ in) in width. Strips can be cut along the length or the width of the fabric but care should be taken to ensure any pattern on the fabric runs in the direction required.

To cut fabric into strips for patchwork proceed as follows:

1 Measure along the edge of the fabric and mark the required widths with a pencil or small scissor cut.

2 Using a ruler and pencil (chalk pencil on dark fabrics) draw parallel lines across the fabric from the initial width markings. Use the fabric weave to keep the lines straight.

3 Cut along the pencil lines.

It is possible to tear some fabrics into strips and this can be a quick and convenient method of producing strips of constant width. However, not all fabrics can be torn successfully without distortion of the pattern or weave. Before tearing any fabric into strips, try an inch or so in one corner. If the pattern or weave distorts then use your scissors and cut it.

All strips, whether cut or torn, should be pressed carefully before beginning to piece the patchwork.

Shape required

Position for cutting out

55 Cutting out asymmetrical shapes

Cutting out for strip patterns

Quilt pieced in multi-coloured ▶ squares of flannel and similar heavy-weight fabrics. Made in Northumberland around 1900 by Sybil Heslop. Though hand-pieced and hand-quilted, the edges of this quilt are machined, a feature of many North-Country quilts of this period

Overleaf
Bedspread.
See pages 108 and 109

56 Stages in marking and cutting out geometrical shapes

(a) Stage 1 and 2
(b) Stage 3

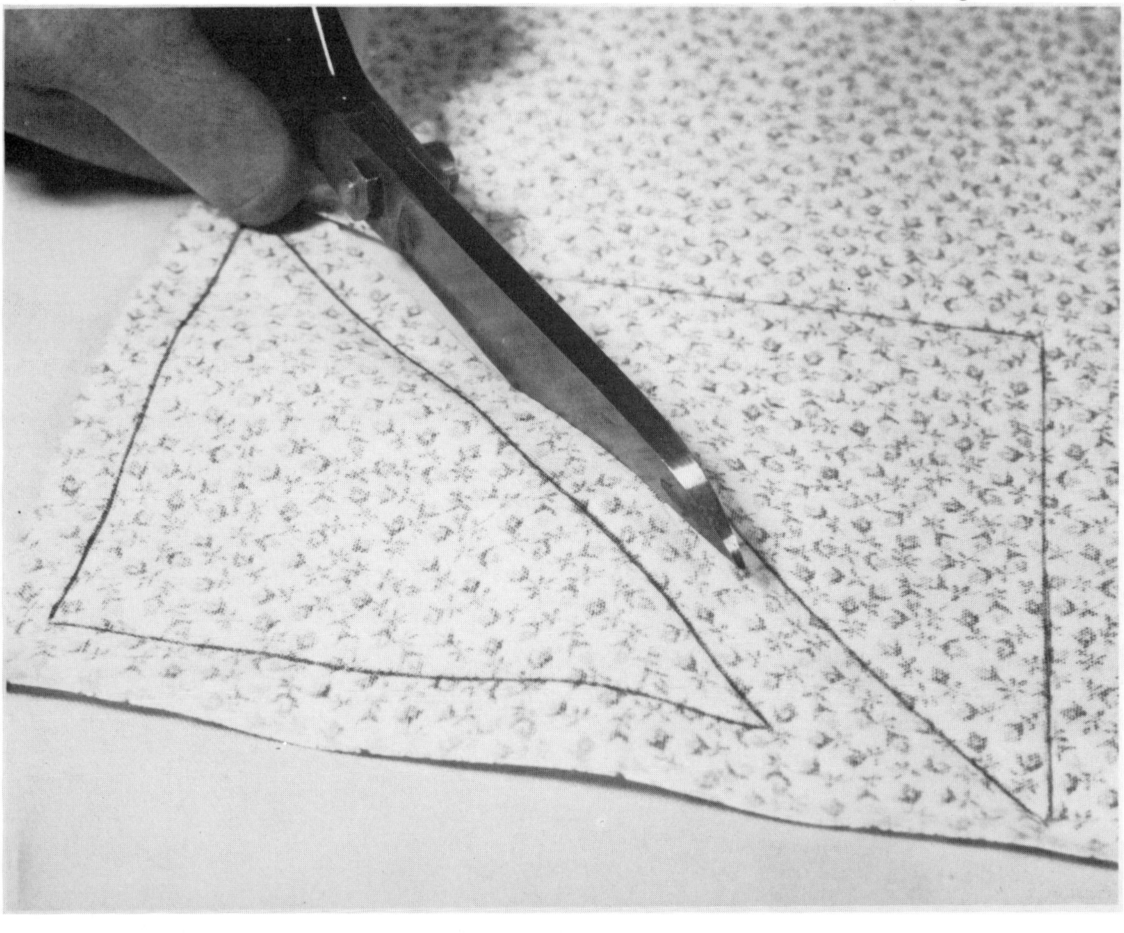

When all the patchwork shapes have been cut out, they should be laid out in the correct order on a flat surface. A table top is fine for a small piece of work or for individual blocks but you may need to get down on your hands and knees on the floor to lay out the patches for a large item like a bedspread. Having done this, you will begin to see how your patterns and colours will look in the finished work and may well be excited at the effects you have created. You may also be just a little puzzled about where to start piecing – which patches to join first, which to join next and so on.

The usual procedure is to join the basic shapes together into groups, eg blocks or strips, then the groups are joined up to complete the patchwork. When piecing by machine, it is best to try and keep all joins as straight-line seams. Figure 58 illustrates how this can be achieved with some of the one-patch patterns.

Block patterns are put together by piecing the individual blocks first then joining the blocks to complete the patchwork. The order for piecing any particular block will vary with the pattern and must be worked out by the individual. The main guide-line is to avoid, where possible, fitting any piece into a sharp angle. The two examples illustrated show different ways of achieving this. In the *Clay's Choice* block (figure 59) the individual patches are joined first into small rectangles, then into squares and then into two large rectangles. These two rectangles are finally joined to complete the block. In the *Bow Tie* block, the four pentagon shapes are added to the central square before their adjoining seams are sewn (see figure 57).

When the completed blocks are ready to be joined they are laid out in position and pieced together into strips. The strips are then joined together and care must be taken to match all the seams carefully. They should be pinned into position and, if necessary, tacked before being stitched together.

You do need to be clear in your mind about the order to follow in piecing your particular patchwork pattern before sewing any patches together. Once you have gained a little experience with patchwork you will soon learn to abstract a pattern visually into the individual shapes and work out how they can be most easily fitted together.

Having worked out the order you can then proceed to pin your shapes together and sew them. The pieces to be joined should be placed right sides together, carefully matching the pencil lines on adjacent sides. Particular attention should be paid to ensuring that the corners of each adjacent piece match well. The pieces can then be pinned together in position. If the pins are placed at right-angles to the seam line, they can be left in position whilst you machine the shapes together.

Once pinned, the shapes are ready to be sewn. This is done by running a line of machine stitching *exactly* along the pencil line on the uppermost shape. Use a stitch setting which gives approximately 5 stitches per centimetre (12 stitches per inch) and

Piecing

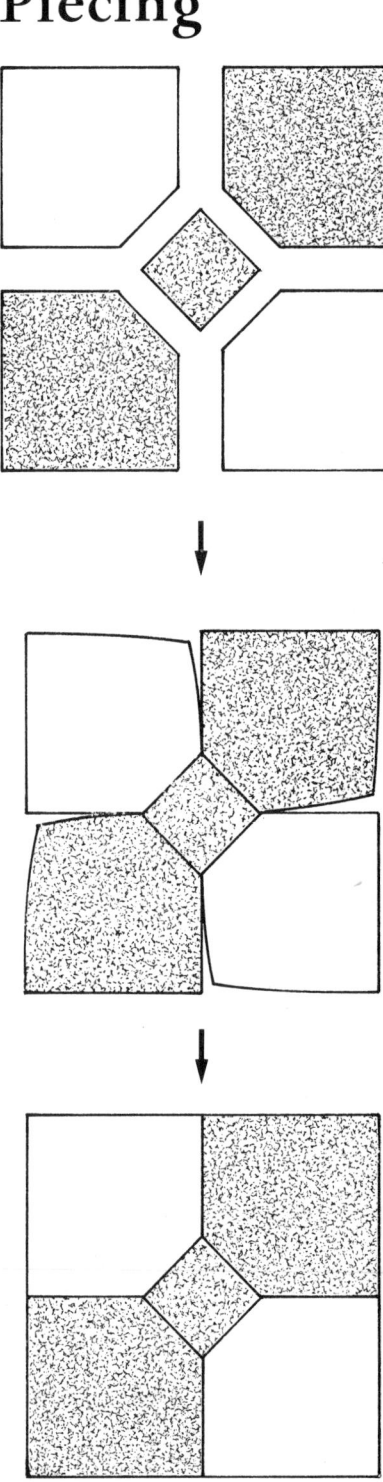

57 Piecing *Bow Tie* block

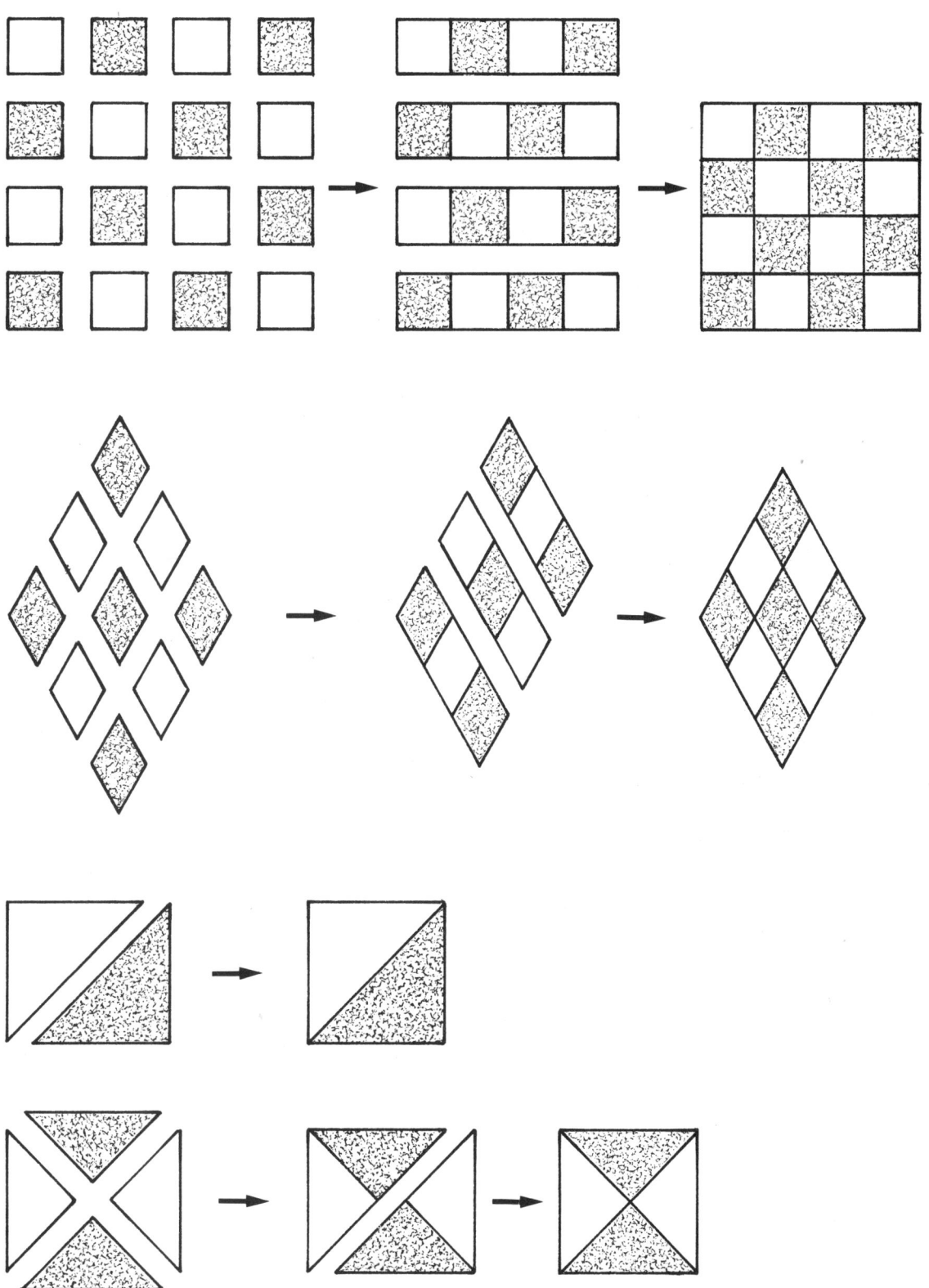

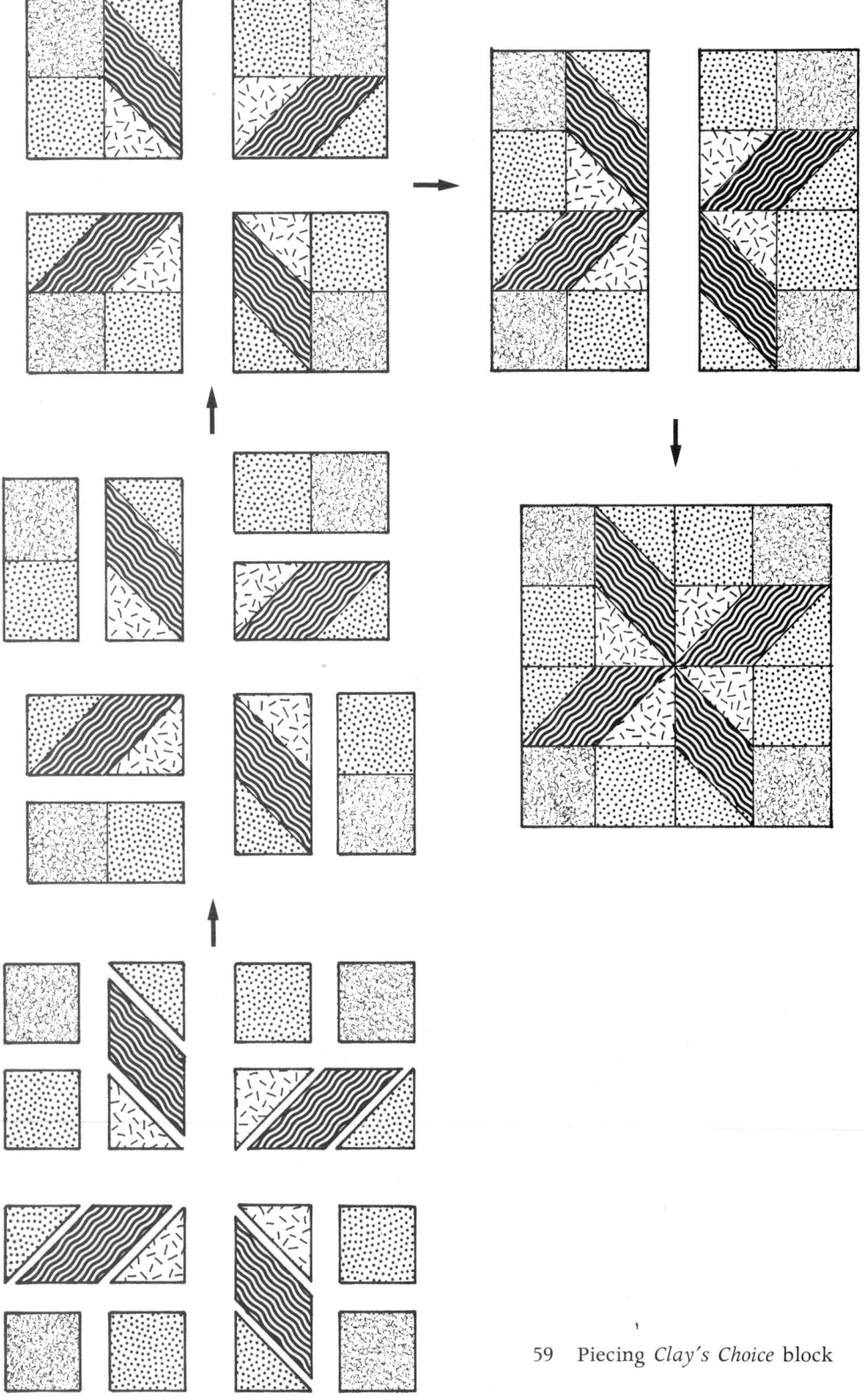

59 Piecing *Clay's Choice* block

always begin and end the seam with a reverse stitch. If you pin together all the patches to be joined in the first stage of piecing, you can sew them all together without cutting the threads after each one. You then end up with a long line of patches dangling over the end of your machine but it keeps them all together and saves time. You only need separate them when you are ready for the next stage of piecing.

After the first seams are completed, they must be pressed before any further joins are made. It is better to press seams to one side rather than press them open. Pressing seams open puts a greater strain on the stitching when the patchwork is in use. Press the seams of one block or unit in the opposite direction to the block or unit it is to be joined to. This avoids excess bulk at any one particular point. It may, however, also be necessary to trim away surplus seam allowance. Where possible, press seams towards a darker fabric to avoid the seam allowance showing through light fabric.

The stages to follow when piecing geometrical shapes can be summed up as follows:

1   Pin shapes, right sides together, matching pencil lines (figure 60a).
2   Machine down pencil line on uppermost shape beginning and ending with a reverse stitch (figure 60b).
3   Repeat for all shapes to be joined in the first stage (figure 60c).
4   Press all seams (figure 60d).
5   Repeat the process until the patchwork is complete. Remember to press seams in alternate directions on adjacent patches.

60   Stages in piecing geometrical shapes

(a) Stage 1

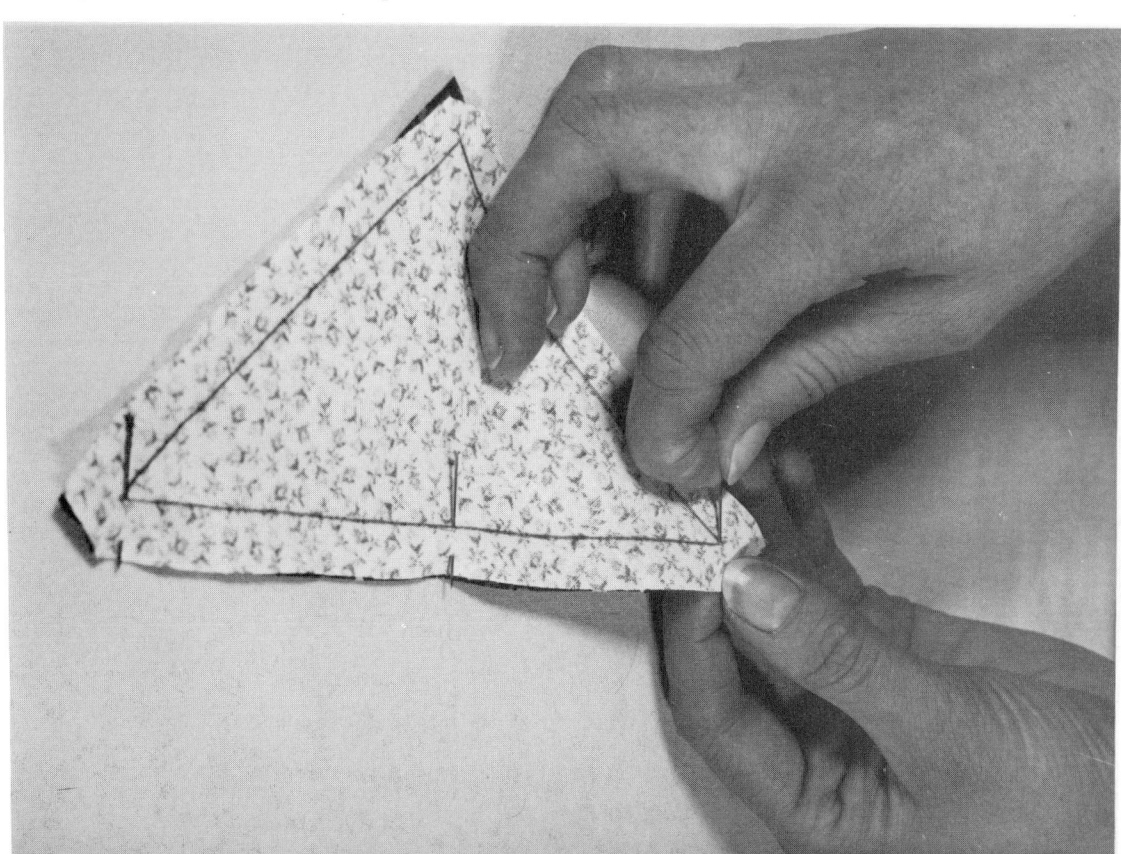

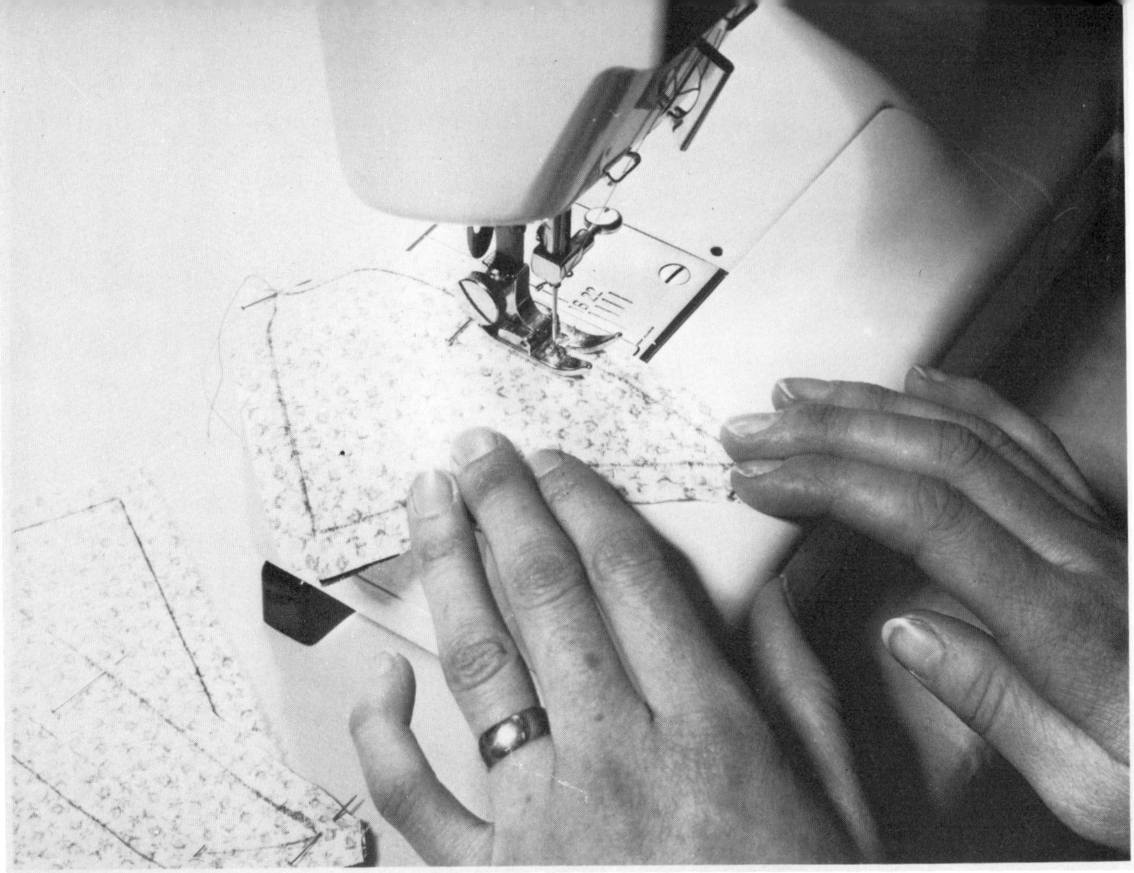

(b) Stage 2
(c) Stage 3

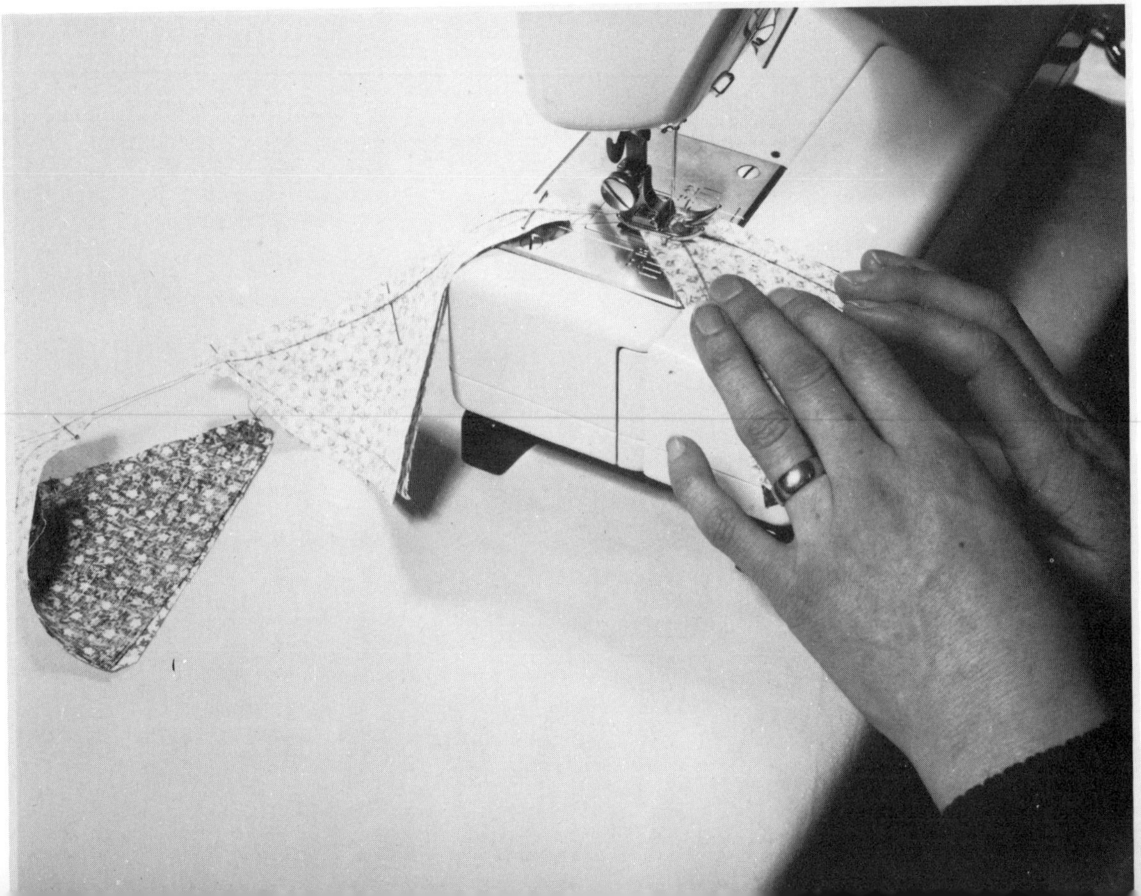

(d) Stage 4
(e) Stage 5

Top-stitching geometrical shapes

When geometrical shapes are top-stitched together, the machine stitching will show on the surface of the patchwork. It takes some thought and skill to ensure that the stitching adds to rather than detracts from the patchwork pattern. One method is to use a zigzag or machine embroidery stitch rather than a straight stitch. If this is done, it is often advisable to use the same colour thread throughout, whatever the colour of the individual patches, to unify the work.

Some particularly beautiful examples of top-stitching used in patchwork can be seen in the work of Eng Tow illustrated in figures 30, 37 and 38. Here the fabric is tucked or pleated and top-stitched. The combined effect is quite different from conventional patchwork.

To top-stitch geometric shapes together, draw the shapes out using templates on the *right* side of the fabric and cut out. Instead of pinning the shapes right sides together, fold over the seam allowance of one patch and pin down in position on the adjacent patch, as in figure 61. Top-stitch along the folded edge on the right side of the fabric.

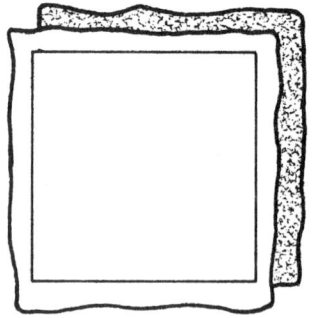

Cut two patches for each shape

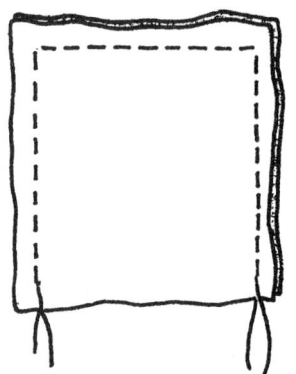

Sew together along three sides

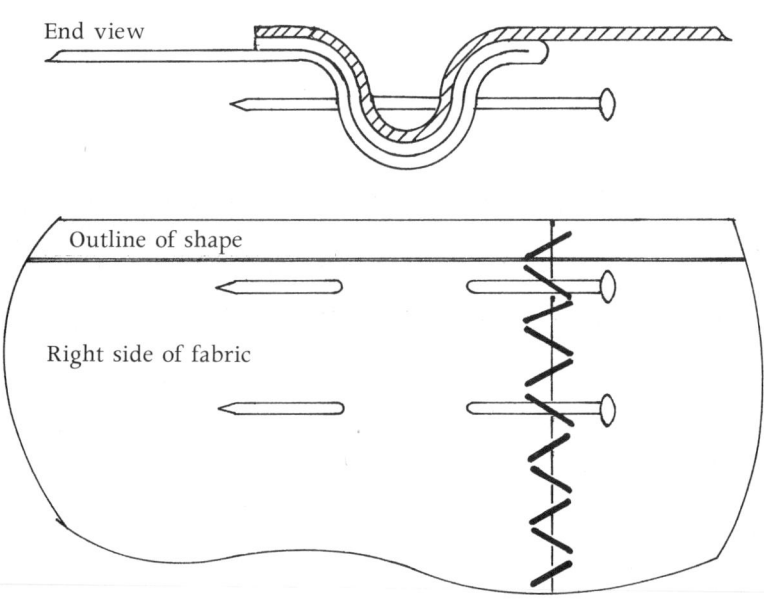

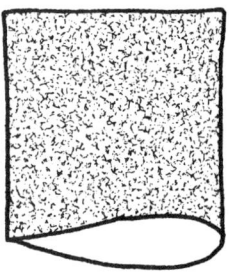

Turn right side out stuff

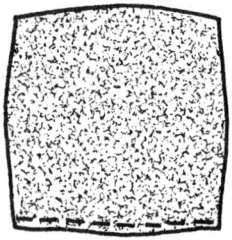

Top-stitch along remaining edge

61   Pinning shapes for top-stitching

62   Stages in making puff patchwork

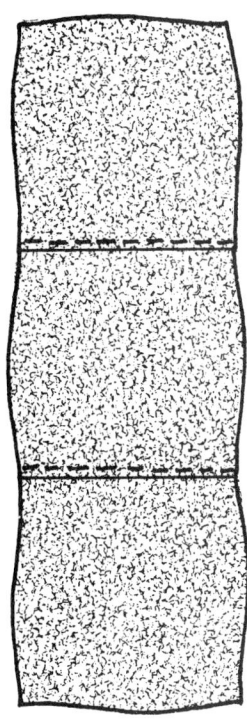

Oversew or top-stitch patches together

Puff patchwork

Puff patchwork, where the individual shapes are padded before being pieced, is usually made with simple shapes like squares and rectangles and combined in one-patch patterns. *Two* fabric patches are cut out for each shape in the pattern in the same way as for any geometrical shape. These two pieces are then sewn together, with a flat seam, on the wrong side of the fabric on all but one side of the shape. The shape is then turned right side out and stuffed through the open side with wadding. When sufficient wadding has been inserted, the open side is sewn up by folding in the edges and top-stitching or hand-sewing. The padded shapes are then pieced together by either oversewing or top-stitching onc to another.

If an even puffier patchwork is required, the patch for the topside is cut to a larger size than the underside piece. The edges of the larger patch are then gathered or tucked (usually one tuck per side) to fit the corresponding sides of the underside patch. The two patches are sewn together, stuffed and completed in the same way as described in figure 62. The very pretty crib lining and quilt illustrated in figure 63 were made in this way.

63   Crib lining and quilt in puff patchwork squares made by Diane Marshall in Liberty prints

Cutting shapes from pieced strips

The method of piecing long strips then cutting large shapes from the strips provides a quick and simple method of piecing patterns like *Rail Fence, Roman Stripe* and even *Spider Web*. Long strips of fabric are cut then the required number of strips are sewn together in long lengths. Templates are made and used to cut out the shapes in the same way as any geometrical shape. The pieced strips are, in effect, treated as a striped fabric and the templates positioned so that the required pattern appears when the shapes are joined.

Swastika (Rail Fence variation)

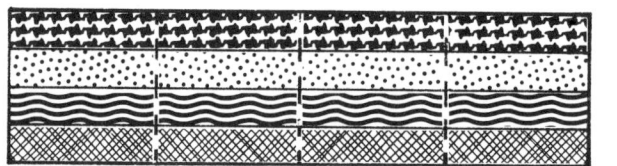

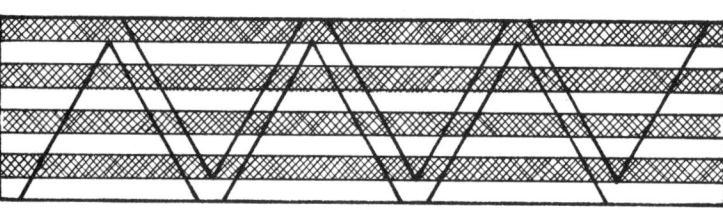

Spider Web

64   Cutting shapes from pieced strips

Piecing onto foundation cloth

Crazy patchwork

Crazy patchwork differs from other patchwork because the individual pieces of fabric do not have to be cut and sewn to any particular shape. They can be as big or as small as you like and as irregular as you choose. Crazy patchwork is, therefore, ideal for scrap patchwork because all shapes and sizes of fabric scraps can be used. However, colours and fabrics still need to be carefully selected for Crazy work. Try, also, to keep a balanced look to your work and avoid shapes which are too regular in outline.

The steps to follow in piecing Crazy patchwork are:

1   Cut foundation cloth to the required size including an amount for seam allowance. Pin first patch either in the centre or at one corner of the cloth.

2   Take second patch, fold over raw edge and tack this over raw edge of first piece overlapping about 1 cm ($\frac{3}{8}$ in).

3   Continue tacking pieces in position laying folded edges of each new piece over raw edges of preceding pieces until the surface of the foundation cloth is covered.

4   Machine along all tacked edges using chosen stitch. Remove tacking stitches.

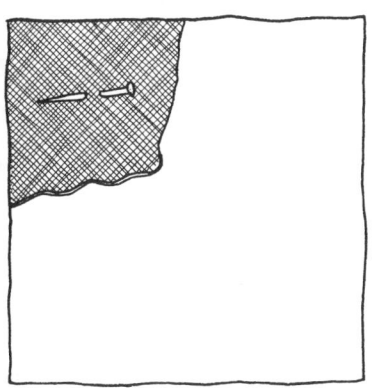

65 Bedspread in squares cut from pieced strips made by Janet Jacobson in green cotton prints

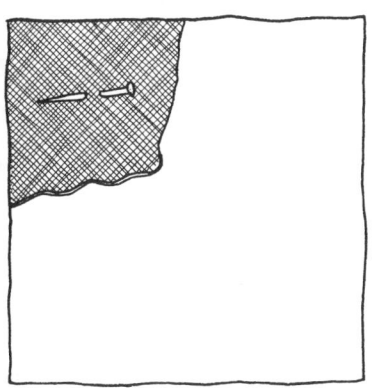
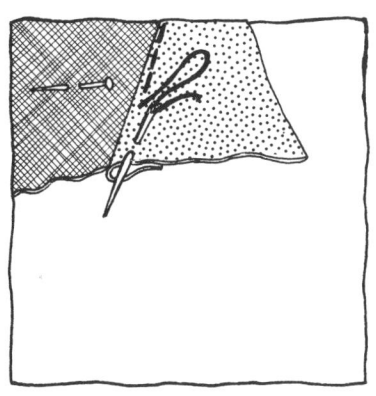
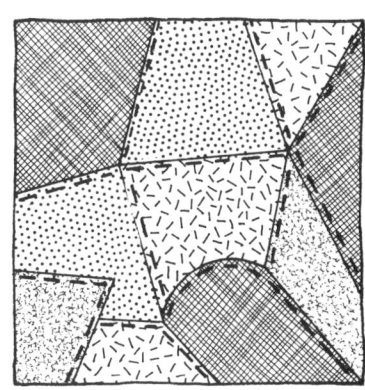

First patch pinned

Second patch tacked in position

All patches tacked ready for top-stitching

66 Piecing *Crazy* patchwork

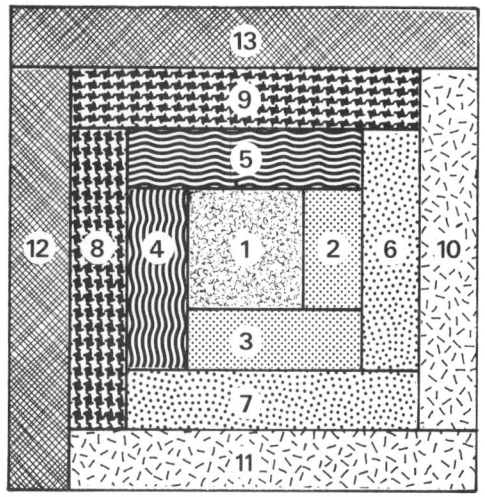

Log Cabin

Courthouse Steps

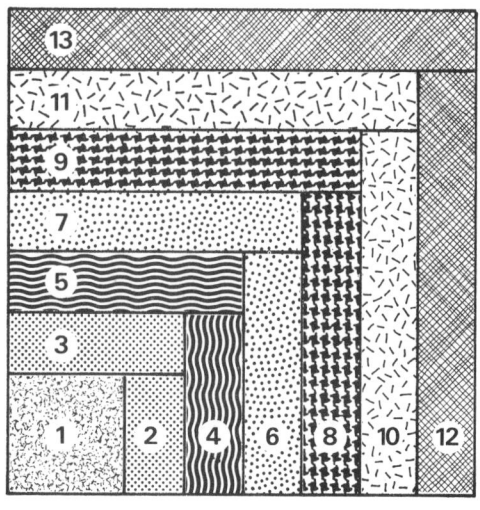

Log Cabin variation

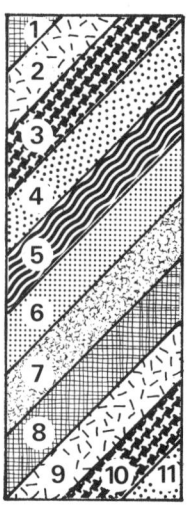

Diagonal Stripe

Simple Stripe

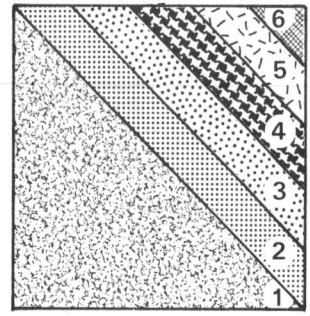

Triangle and Stripes

67 Order for piecing strip patterns

Piecing strip patterns

The method for piecing all the various strip patterns onto foundation cloth is the same in principle. The first piece of fabric is pinned in position, the second piece placed alongside it with right sides together and raw edges matching. The two pieces are then sewn together through the foundation cloth about 6 mm ($\frac{1}{4}$ in) in from the raw edge. The second piece is turned over and pinned into position. All subsequent pieces are pieced in this manner. A straight machine stitch is used with a setting of about 4 stitches per centimetre (10 stitches per inch). In practice, the size and shape of the patches, the sequence adopted when piecing and whether you begin from a corner or a central position will bring out the pattern variations. A few of the many strip patterns which can be sewn on foundation cloth are illustrated in figure 67.

The following instructions for piecing a *Log Cabin* block will illustrate how to proceed with piecing strip patterns. If you have followed the instructions for marking the *Log Cabin* block given on page 68, the block can be pieced as follows:

1 Cut out the fabric piece for the centre square. This should be the finished size of the square plus 6 mm ($\frac{1}{4}$ in) all round for seam allowance. Pin this piece centrally in position on the foundation cloth, right side uppermost. (Figure 68a)

2 Taking fabric for first strip, lay this along one side of the centre square, right sides together and matching raw edges. The guideline marked on the foundation fabric should show above the positioned strip and indicate the sewing line. Machine strip in position. (Figure 68b)

3 Cut off surplus, turn over first strip and pin. (Figure 68c)

4 Turn through 90° to the next side of the centre square. Position second strip in the same way as the first ensuring that this strip also covers the previous strip sewn. Machine into position, cut off surplus, turn over and pin. (Figure 68d)

5 Piece third and fourth strips in the same way on the next two sides of the centre square to complete one round. (Figure 68e)

6 Complete the required number of rounds of strips for the chosen block. (Figure 68f)

Using wadding as foundation cloth

It is possible to piece directly onto terylene wadding using the wadding (batting) as foundation cloth. However, the wadding cannot be marked out so, to ensure that each strip is sewn in the correct position, it needs to be measured the correct distance away from the previous one. The tea-cosy for which instructions are given on page 96 is made in this way and the detailed instructions for that will indicate how this is done.

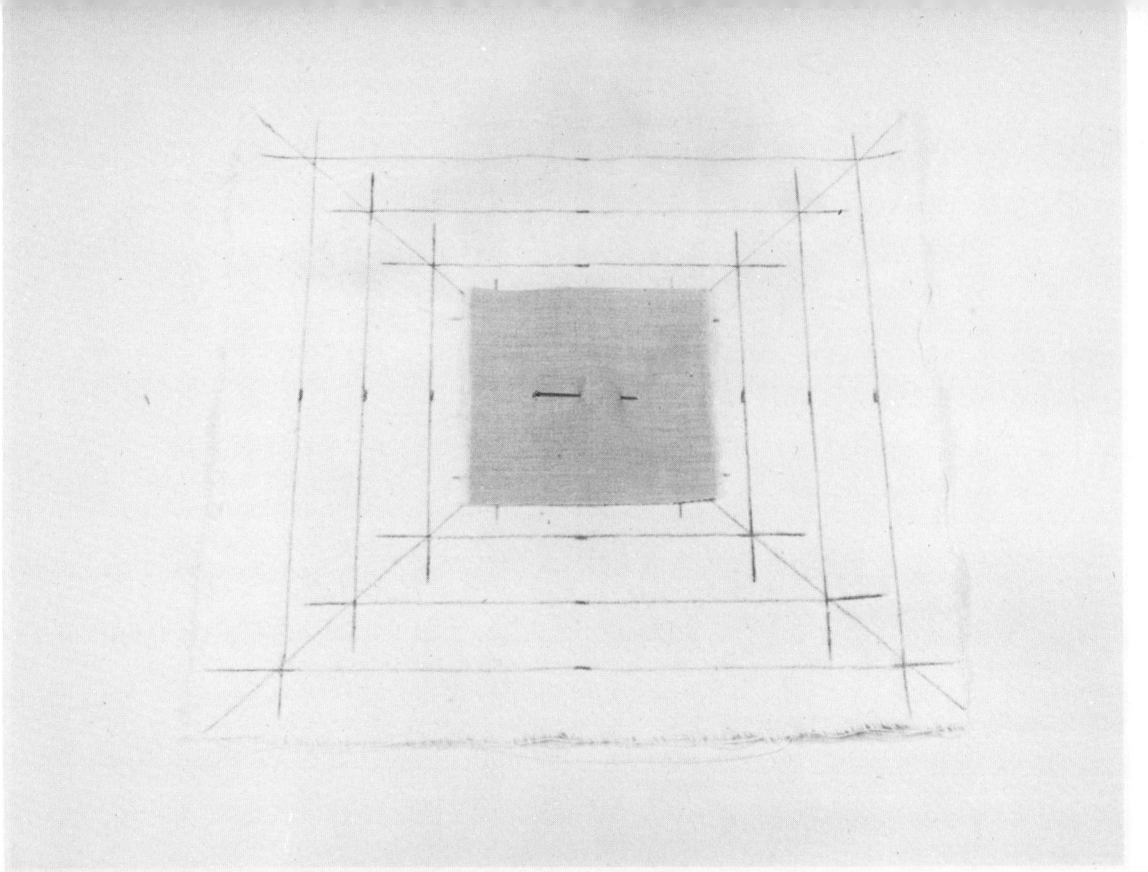

68   Stages in piecing a *Log Cabin* block

(a) Stage 1
(b) Stage 2

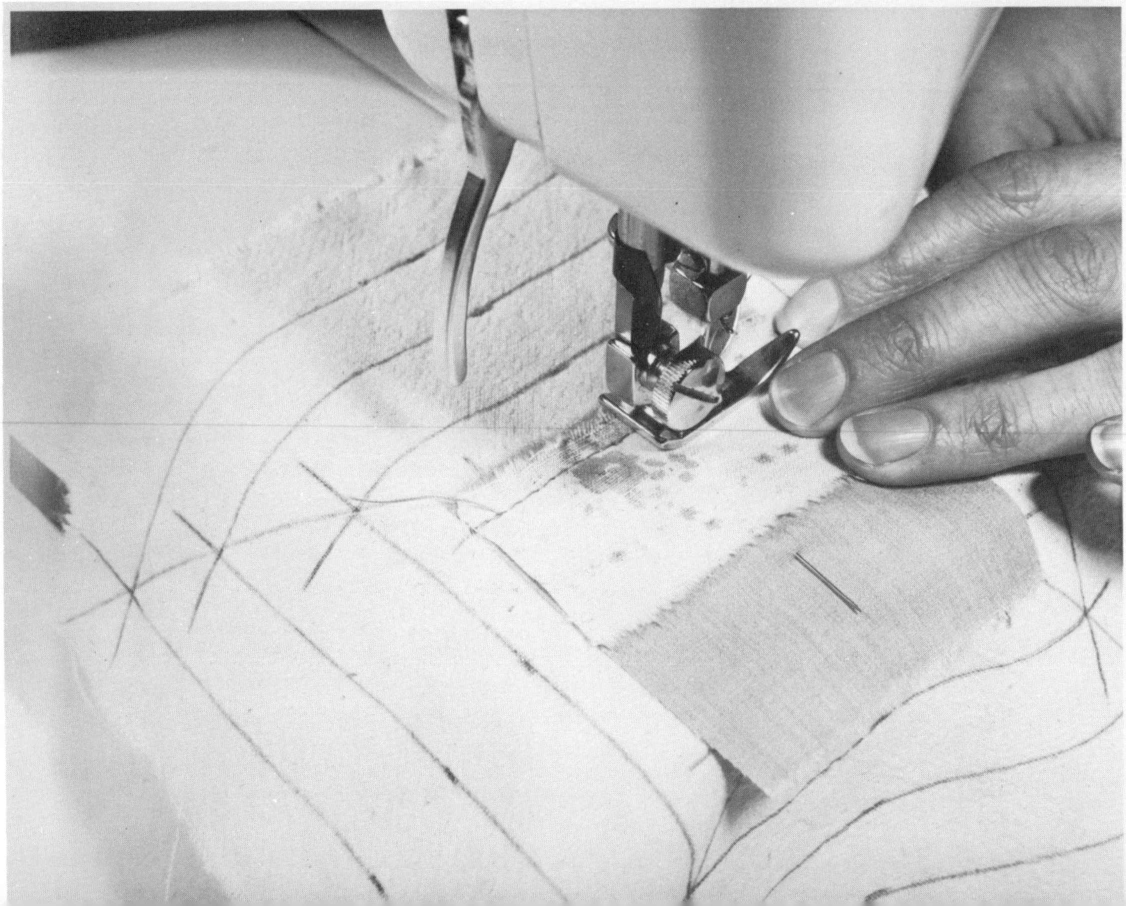

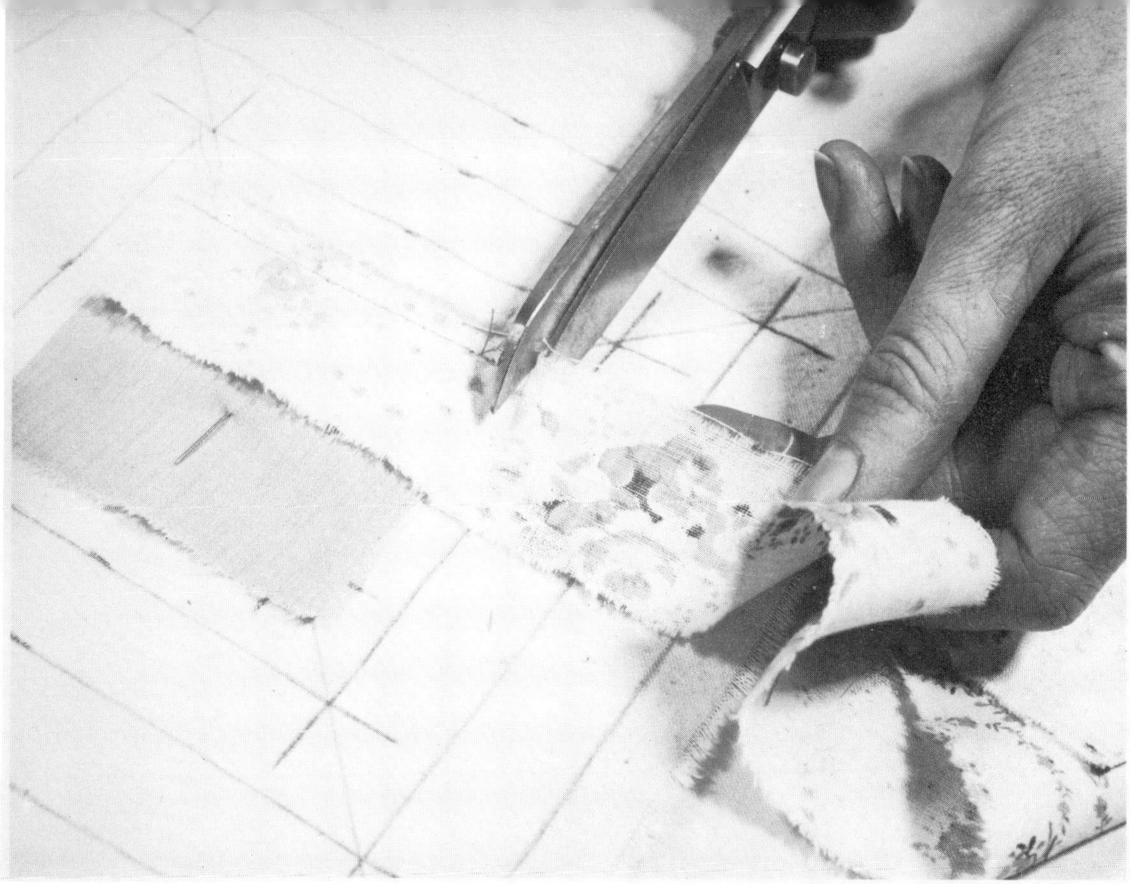

(c) Stage 3
(d) Stage 4

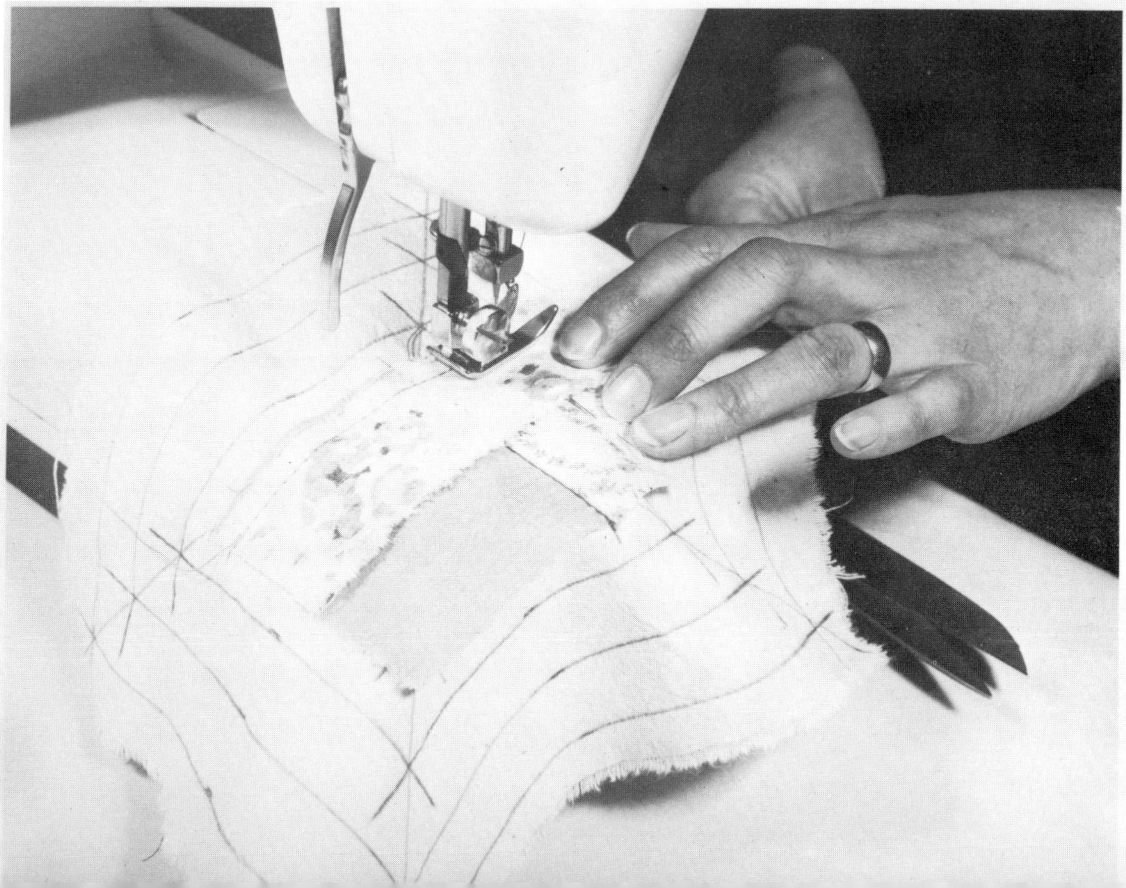

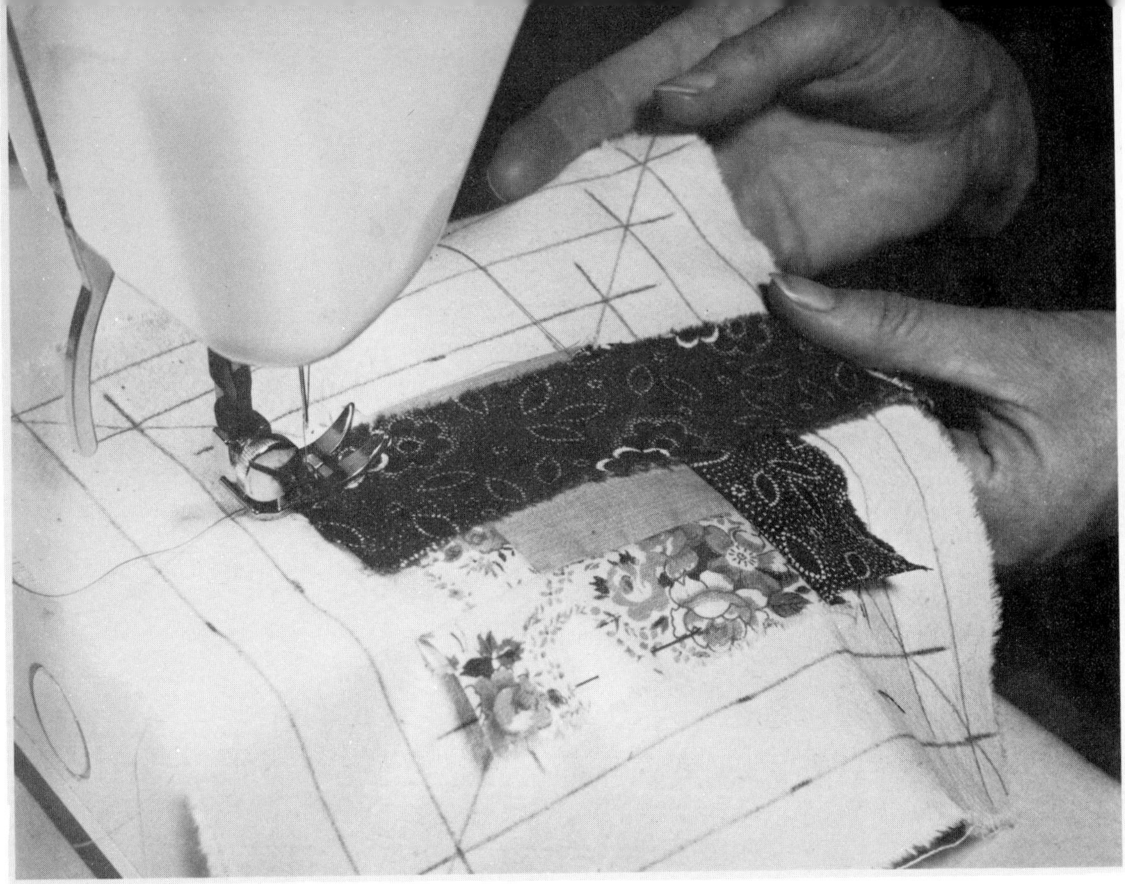

(e) Stage 5
(f) Stage 6

Finishing

Once your patchwork is complete it is ready to be finished and made up into the appropriate article. Do not spoil a good piece of patchwork with bad finishing. Take as much care with the finishing as with the patchwork itself.

Borders

You may wish to add a border – perhaps to a cushion, bedspread or hanging. A border can have two functions; firstly, it can frame the patchwork and add to the appearance of the design and, secondly, it can make up the size to the required dimensions. Borders can be either plain or patterned fabric strips or they can be patchwork borders pieced in a design which complements the main patchwork. If fabric strips are used they should be cut following the straight grain of the fabric and not on the bias. If it is not possible to cut the full length of a strip out of one piece of fabric, try and position any joins centrally or in the same positions on either side. Patchwork borders are pieced together in the same way as the main patchwork.

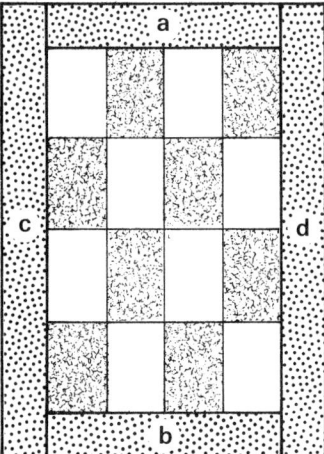

69   Square cut borders

Square cut borders
For square cut borders, two border strips (a and b) are cut to correspond to the width of the patchwork. These are machined to the top and bottom of the patchwork, right sides together, and pressed flat. Two further strips (c and d) are then cut corresponding to the length of the patchwork plus the width of strips a and b. The strips c and d are then machined to the sides of the patchwork and to the edges of strips a and b, right sides together, and pressed flat.

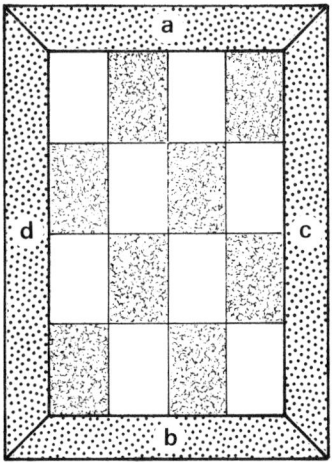

Mitred borders
For mitred borders, four strips (a, b, c and d) are cut corresponding to the lengths of the sides and adding twice the width of the strips to each length. These strips are tacked in position along the edges of the patchwork, right sides together, allowing the amount corresponding to the width of the strips to extend at each end. The strips are then machined along each edge from corner to corner. The overlap at each end of each strip is then folded to give a diagonal edge and pressed firmly. The pressed edges at each corner are carefully matched and the crease used as the sewing line for the corner (see figure 70). Once sewn, the excess fabric can be cut away and the borders pressed flat.

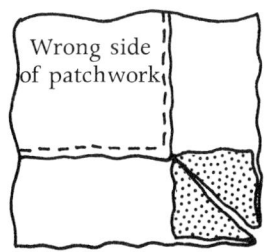

Corners folded for mitre

70   Mitred borders

Border strips with corner squares
This is the type of border so frequently seen in the framed or medallion quilts. Four strips (a, b, c and d) are cut corresponding to the four sides of the patchwork. Four squares (e, f, g and h) are cut with sides corresponding to the widths of the strips. Squares e

and f are machined, right sides together, to the edges of strip a and squares g and h machined to strip b in the same way. These two strips are then machined in position on the patchwork and pressed. The edges of strips d and c are then attached to squares e and g and f and h respectively. Strips d and c are then machined in position on the patchwork and any excess seam allowance cut away and the corners snipped.

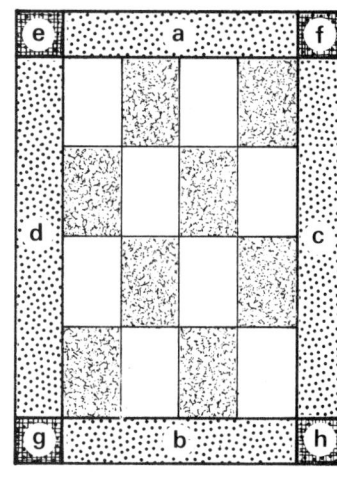

71   Border strips with corner squares

Most patchwork will need to be lined to cover the wrong side of the work and to give 'body' to the work. If the patchwork is to be quilted then the wadding is placed between the patchwork top and the lining.

A lining can be attached by cutting a piece of fabric to the size of the finished patchwork including an amount for seam allowance. This is placed with the patchwork on a flat surface, right sides together, and the two layers carefully smoothed together. The two layers should then be tacked along the edge and machined along three sides. The tacking stitches are then removed, the work turned right side out and the remaining edge completed by oversewing or top-stitching.

Linings

A lining can also be attached by sewing a binding strip along the edge (see page 92). If this is required, the patchwork and lining are placed wrong sides together and tacked with rows of long tacking stitches, at intervals of about 30 cm (12 in). This tacking is also done if the work is to be quilted to hold the layers together. The binding strips are then attached as illustrated in figure 73.

If the patchwork is not to be quilted then the lining should be held fast to the patchwork top at appropriate points on large pieces of work. This is known as tying. If the lining is not tied to the patchwork it will sag underneath and probably wrinkle.

Tying

There are several ways tying can be done. The commonest method is to knot the two layers together with either reef knots or french knots using a strong cotton thread such as crochet cotton. Do not use synthetic thread – it will not hold in a knot. Alternatively, a decorative embroidery stitch can be used, eg satin stitch or cross stitch. The process of tying is open to individual interpretation but should be neatly and securely done and, if the ties are visible on the surface of the patchwork, they should not spoil the design.

Tying can also be done to hold a layer of wadding in place as an alternative to quilting.

72 Quilted wall hanging – strip pattern with mitred borders and
contrast binding strip to hold lining and patchwork top together.
Made by the author by machining polyester-cotton strips onto
terylene wadding

Binding strips can be used to finish off a piece of patchwork in addition to borders and also to secure the lining and patchwork edges together. Binding strips should be cut along the fabric weave – only use bias strips if they are to be attached around a curved edge. Like borders, try and keep any joins central or in the same positions either side. Attach binding strips to the top and bottom of the patchwork by machining along the edge, right sides together. Fold over the strips to the wrong side and hem into position. Attach the strips to the remaining two sides in the same way ensuring that the raw edges of the first two strips are also covered. Oversew the ends.

Binding strips

73 Attaching binding strips

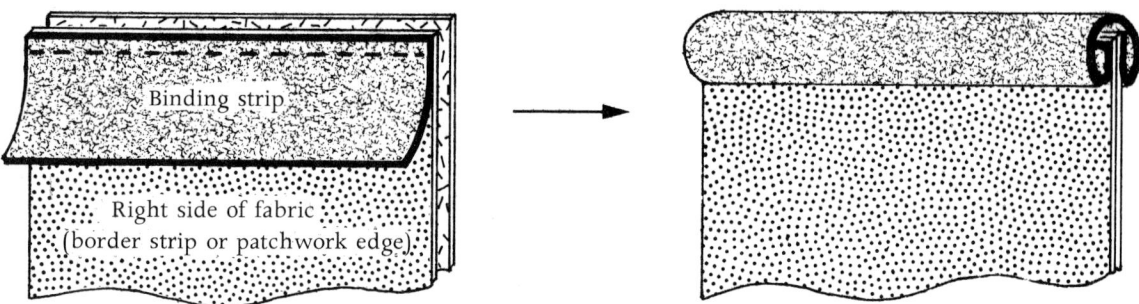

Binding strip

Right side of fabric
(border strip or patchwork edge)

Inserting zips

Zips for cushions, duvet covers and garments can be inserted using the conventional method in dress-making, ie folding over the seam edges, tacking the zip in position and top-stitching. However, this method can be difficult with patchwork sewn onto foundation cloth because of the greater bulk of fabric on the patchwork side. It becomes almost impossible to do well if the work has been quilted or if wadding is used as the foundation fabric.

The alternative is to insert the zip 'invisibly'. This way the two edges to be joined are placed right sides together. The zip is then placed wrong side uppermost between the two edges and tacked in position on top of the fabric edges (see figure 74). The edges are then machined to the zip on the wrong side of the zip, close up against the teeth, using the machine zipper foot, if you have one.

Always insert a zip *before* completing the remaining sides of the work. It is a much simpler process if carried out at this stage.

74 Inserting a zip 'invisibly'

Wrong side of zip

Wrong side of fabric

Step-by-step instructions

All items illustrated in this section were designed and made by the author

The floor cushion is made in 7.6 cm (3 in) squares and the completed size is 68.4 cm (27 in) square. Nine fabrics are required to give a range from the lightest fabric in the corner to the darkest fabric in the centre.

Materials
Nine different fabrics for the patchwork top sufficient to cut two squares of A, four of B, six of C, eight of D, ten of E, twelve of F, fourteen of G, sixteen of H and nine of I
Matching fabric for underside of cushion 71 cm × 71 cm (28 in × 28 in)
Matching zip 61 cm (24 in) long
Matching sewing thread
Cushion pad 70 cm × 70 cm ($27\frac{1}{2}$ in × $27\frac{1}{2}$ in)

Template
Make template 7.6 cm (3 in) square by tracing shape from outline of figure 76, cutting out and mounting on sandpaper or stiff card.

Cutting out
Mark out and cut appropriate number of squares from each fabric leaving 1 cm ($\frac{3}{8}$ in) seam allowance around all squares.

To make up
1 Piece squares together into strips according to figure 76. For strip one, piece together ABCDEFGHI, for strip two, piece together BCDEFGHIH and so on for the nine strips. Press each seam carefully to the side making sure to press seams on adjacent strips in opposite directions.
2 Join strips together, strip one to two, two to three, etc, carefully matching seams. The patchwork will then be complete and should be carefully pressed.
3 Attach zip along one edge of patchwork, positioning it centrally along the edge. Attach other side of zip to fabric for underside (see page 92 – 'Inserting Zips'). Sew short seam either side of zip to complete zip edge and strengthen the inner edges of these seams by a double row of stitching. Undo zip.
4 With right sides together, sew patchwork to underside fabric along remaining three sides with a flat seam. Follow lines on patchwork edge carefully and neaten this seam by over-sewing or zigzag stitch.
5 Press all seams, turn right side out and insert pad.

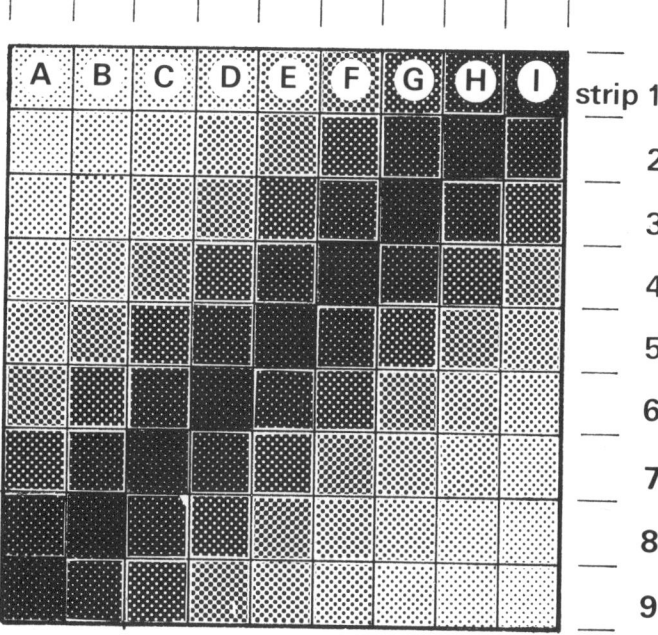

76 Diagram for floor cushion
(use outline for template)

The tea-cosy is made by sewing fabric strips directly onto terylene wadding. The width of the cosy is 32 cm (12½ in), the height is 23.5 cm (9¼ in) and the finished width of each strip is 3.2 cm (1¼ in). It should fit a medium-sized teapot.

Tea-cosy

Materials
20 cm (¼ yd) of two fabrics (A and B) for the patchwork
30 cm (⅓ yd) of fabric for lining
30 cm (⅓ yd) of 113 g (4 oz) terylene wadding
Bias strip or bias binding 61 cm × 2.5 cm (24 in × 1 in)
Matching sewing thread

Pattern
Make paper pattern as illustrated in figure 78.

Cutting out
Using paper pattern, cut out two lining pieces to the exact size of the pattern. Using paper pattern cut out two wadding pieces by adding 2 cm (¾ in) all round curved edge and 1 cm (⅜ in) to base of pattern shape.
Cut patchwork fabrics into strips 4.5 cm (1¾ in) wide.
Press all strips.

To make up
1 Lay strip of fabric A from bottom *left-hand* corner diagonally across wadding, right side up. Pin lightly in position. Cut away surplus.
2 Lay strip of fabric B on top of first strip A, right sides together, and matching lower raw edges. Pin lightly but do not stretch strips. Set machine to a long stitch length and machine along lower raw edges 6 mm (¼ in) in from edge with a straight stitch. Turn second strip (fabric B) over to right side, pin in position and cut away surplus.
3 Lay strip of fabric A on top of second strip, right sides together and matching lower raw edges. Measure across 3.2 cm (1¼ in) from seam joining first two strips and this will give seam line for joining second and third strips. Machine as before, turn over strip A, pin and cut away surplus.

Waistcoat ▶
See pages 100 and 101

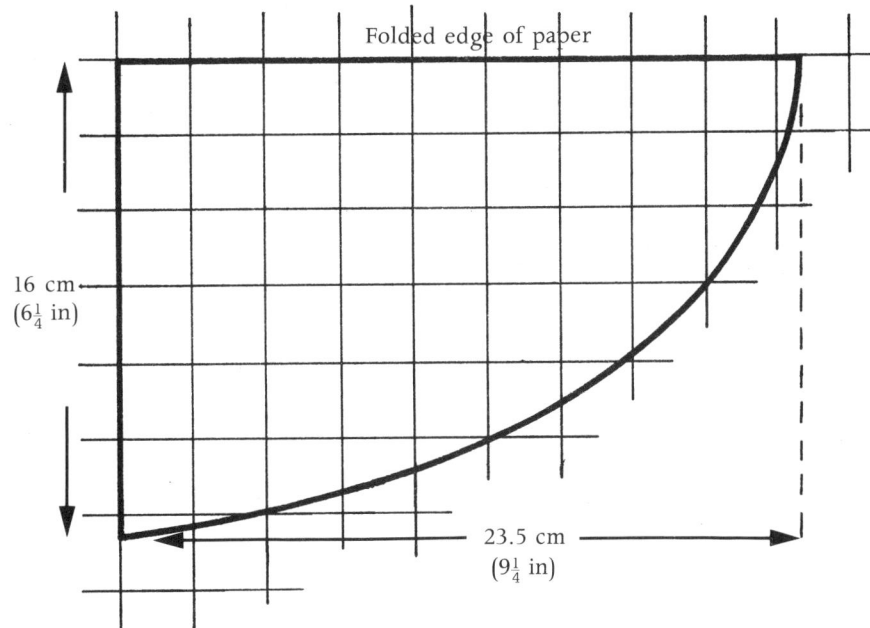

Folded edge of paper

T
O
P

16 cm
($6\frac{1}{4}$ in)

23.5 cm
($9\frac{1}{4}$ in)

78   Pattern diagram for tea-cosy   Each square represents 2.5 cm (1 in) square

4   Continue adding strips in this way, alternating fabrics A
and B and measuring required distance of 3.2 cm ($1\frac{1}{4}$ in)
from each previous seam to ensure each strip finishes the
correct width. When the area below the first strip is
completed, turn the work and complete the top half of the
side to match.

5   Complete the second side of the cosy to match by laying
the first strip on the second side diagonally across from the
bottom *right-hand* corner and continuing to piece as for the
first side.

6   Attach lining by laying lining pieces to the completed
patchwork sides, right sides together, and machining along
base edges 1.5 cm ($\frac{5}{8}$ in) in from edge. Turn lining to inside
and pin along base edge.

7   To complete cosy, lay two sides together with lining inside.
Take paper pattern and cut away 12 mm ($\frac{1}{2}$ in) all round.
Lay this reduced pattern on one side of the cosy, lining up
the pattern base with the base edge and pin in position.
Tack all round the curved edge just outside the paper with
a contrast tacking thread to give a guide-line for attaching
the binding.

8   Attach bias strip by pinning one edge of strip to guide-line
around curve, folding in ends. Tack strip in position and
machine 1 cm ($\frac{3}{8}$ in) in from edge using a straight stitch and
a heavy-weight needle (size 16). Trim away surplus around
curve to 1 cm ($\frac{3}{8}$ in), turn over bias strip and hand-sew into
position.

◀ *Duvet cover*
See pages
102 and 103

The patchwork borders on these table mats are pieced in the Goose-wing pattern. The finished size of each mat is 35.5 cm × 25.5 cm (14 in × 10 in).

Set of table mats

Materials
1.10 m (1¼ yd) of fabric 90 cm (36 in) wide or 90 cm (1 yd) of fabric 120 cm (48 in) wide for bases and centre panels
Scraps of fabric for patchwork borders
Matching sewing thread

Templates
Make templates for the two triangles by tracing outlines from figure 80, cutting out and mounting on sandpaper or stiff card.

Cutting out
From main fabric cut out four base pieces 38 cm × 28 cm (15 in × 11 in) and four centre panels 25.5 cm × 28 cm (10 in × 11 in).
From scraps for borders cut sixty-four large triangles and one hundred and twenty-eight small triangles leaving 6 mm (¼ in) seam allowance around triangles.

To make up
1 Make up patchwork borders by piecing two small triangles to each large triangle as in figure 81. Combine all the triangles into sixty-four strip units in this way. Piece together eight strip units for each border. Press carefully.
2 Sew patchwork border to each side of the centre panel with a 12 mm (½ in) seam allowance on the centre panel and following the seam lines drawn on the patchwork shapes. Press.
3 With right sides together, sew base piece to top along two side edges, across top and across the patchwork border along the base, carefully following the seam lines on the patchwork pieces. Open out, turn in edge along base of centre panel and oversew.

NOTE If you wish to add more insulation to the mats and/or quilt them, cut a piece of terylene wadding 56 g or 85 g (2 oz or 3 oz) the finished size for each mat. When sewing base to top, leave base edge open and slip wadding inside before oversewing. Quilt if required.

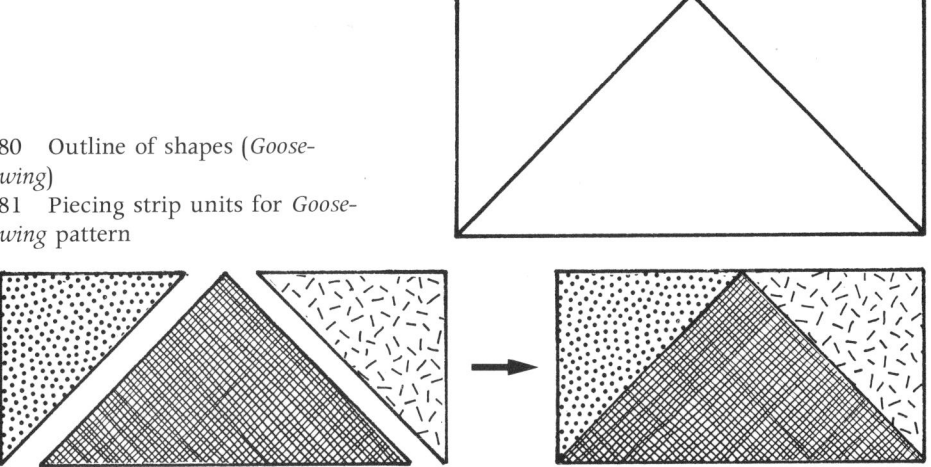

80   Outline of shapes (*Goose-wing*)
81   Piecing strip units for *Goose-wing* pattern

See colour plate facing page 96
The waistcoat is made by top-stitching patchwork pieces in the crazy patchwork style onto terylene wadding. The pattern given will fit a 90 cm (36 in) bust size. To make larger or smaller, add or cut away from side seams.

Materials
1.10 m ($1\frac{1}{4}$ yd) of fabric 90 cm (36 in) wide for lining
1.10 m ($1\frac{1}{4}$ yd) of 113 g (4 oz) terylene wadding 90 cm (36 in) wide
Fabric for patchwork totalling 1.50 m ($1\frac{5}{8}$ yd)
7 m (8 yd) of matching binding tape 2.5 cm (1 in) wide
Matching sewing thread

Pattern
Make paper pattern for back and two sides following figure 82. Alternately, use a dress-making pattern but avoid using one with darts.

Cutting out
Using paper pattern, cut out lining pieces for two sides and back to exact size of pattern (which includes seam allowance). Using paper pattern, cut out wadding pieces for two sides and back adding 1.5 cm ($\frac{5}{8}$ in) all round to allow for shrinking as patchwork is sewn.

To make up
1 Iron all fabrics for patchwork.
2 Starting in the centre or at the side of each wadding piece (two sides and back), cut irregularly-shaped patches from the chosen fabrics and piece onto the wadding. Begin by pinning first piece in position, cut second piece, fold over raw edge and tack in position. Continue cutting and tacking pieces in position until all the wadding is covered and no raw edges are exposed except at the outside edges of the front and back pieces. Top-stitch along the tacked edges of each patch using either a straight stitch, zigzag stitch or embroidery stitch according to choice. Where it is necessary to stop or start a seam in the middle of a piece, start and finish with a reverse stitch and cut threads as close as possible to stitching. Try to maintain symmetry of the two sides by using the same fabrics in roughly the same positions on the patchwork.
3 When patchwork is complete, pin sides and shoulder seams. If possible, try on the garment and adjust seams as required. Sew side and shoulder seams with a flat seam. Trim to 6 mm ($\frac{1}{4}$ in) and press.
4 Sew side and shoulder seams of lining with a flat seam adjusting as required to fit patchwork.

5 With wrong sides together, pin lining to inside of waistcoat all round raw edges of armholes, neck, front opening and base. Tack all round.

6 Attach binding to all edges, machining onto right side 1 cm ($\frac{3}{8}$ in) away from edge. Turn over and oversew to lining on inside.

7 Make ties by cutting eight lengths of binding 23 cm (9 in) long. Fold in half, turn in edges and oversew or top-stitch along all edges. Sew ends of ties in position on waistcoat.

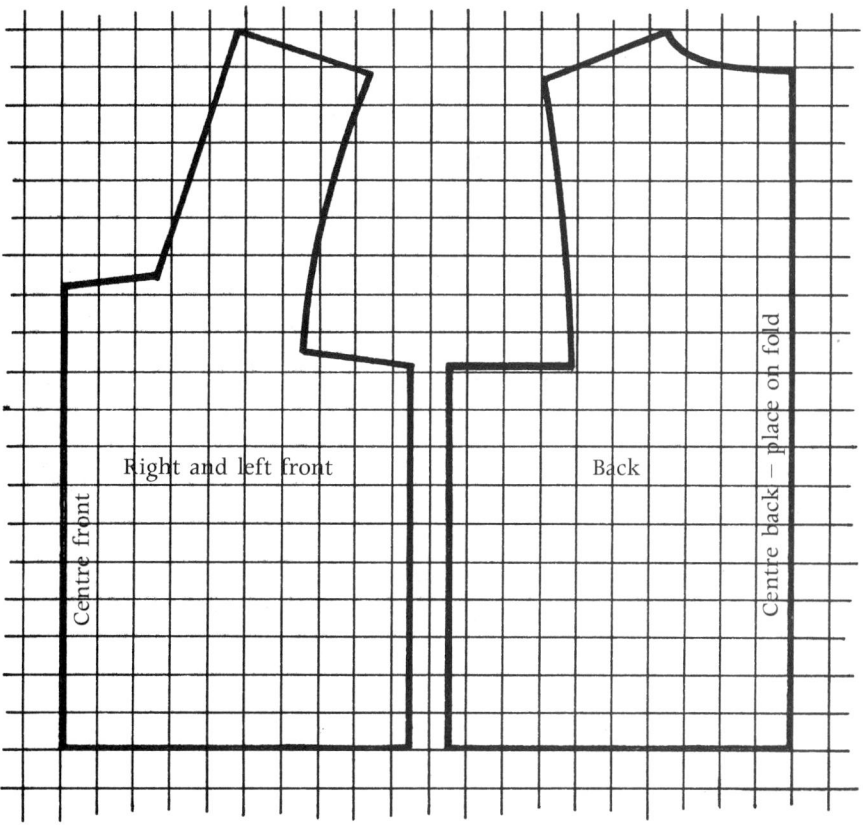

Each square represents 2.5 cm (1 in) square

82 Pattern diagram for waistcoat

Duvet cover

The duvet cover is made in the block style using the block pattern known as *World Without End*. The completed size is 122 cm × 183 cm (48 in × 72 in) to fit a standard single size duvet. This particular block is one in which a circular pattern is created when four blocks are pieced together and interesting optical effects can be obtained with a carefully chosen colour scheme. Each block is 30.5 cm (12 in) square and there are twenty-four blocks in all.

Materials

For patchwork 60 cm (24 in) of fabric 90 cm (36 in) wide for squares, 2.50 m ($2\frac{3}{4}$ yd) of 90 cm (36 in) wide fabric for tall triangles and 3.20 m ($3\frac{1}{2}$ yd) of 90 cm (36 in) wide fabric for wide triangles
Length of cotton sheeting 127 cm × 188 cm (74 in × 50 in) for underside of cover
Lining fabric 127 cm × 188 cm (74 in × 50 in) if required
Two matching 51 cm (20 in) zips
Matching sewing thread

Templates

Make templates for the three shapes by tracing outlines from figure 83. Note – only half the shape is given for the wide triangle, so place on folded paper and cut out full shape. Cut out shapes and mount on sandpaper or stiff card.

Cutting out

Cut out twenty-four squares, ninety-six tall triangles and ninety-six wide triangles from chosen fabrics leaving 1 cm ($\frac{3}{8}$ in) seam allowance around all shapes.

To make up

1 Piece each block by following the order given in figure 84. Press all seams carefully.
2 Join blocks into six strips of four blocks each.
3 Join strips carefully matching seams to complete the patchwork.
4 Attach two zips at lower edge of patchwork making sure that both zips close at the centre. Attach zips to correct edge of underside fabric. Make short flat seam at either end of zips to complete this edge.
5 Lay patchwork top on flat surface with underside fabric on top, right sides together. If a lining is also to be attached, lay this on top of the underside fabric. Carefully smooth all layers together and pin along three remaining edges. Tack layers together and then machine carefully following seam lines on patchwork shapes. If lining has been included,

turn this over to cover the patchwork side and oversew to the zip edge on the inside.

6 Turn cover right side out and press.

83   Outline of shapes (*World Without End*)

Place on fold of paper

Actual size

84   Piecing *World Without End* block

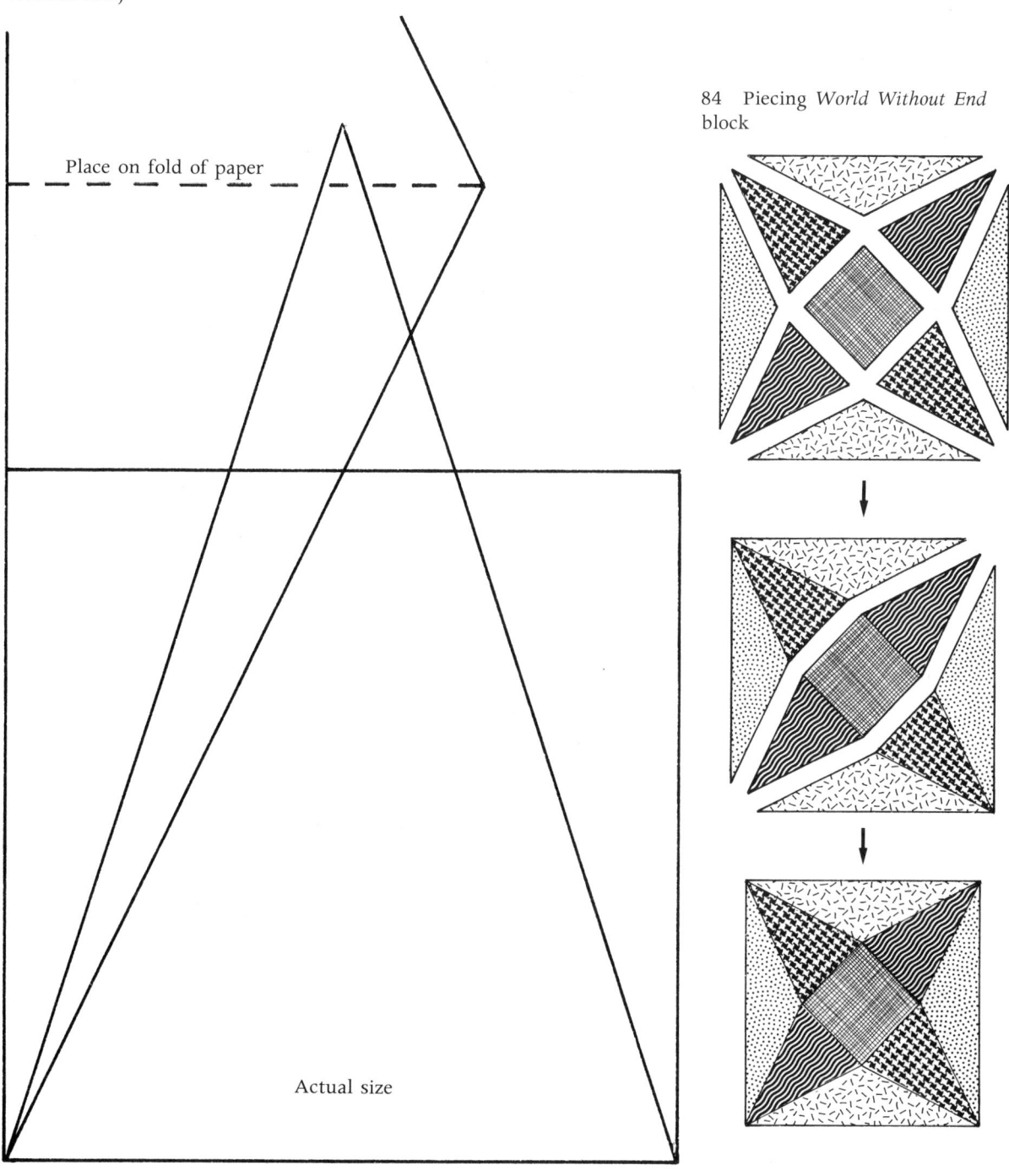

The scatter cushion is made in the *Pineapple* pattern, a variation of *Log Cabin*. Strips of fabric are sewn onto foundation fabric around the central square and corner triangles added to complete the patchwork. The cushion is 43 cm × 43 cm (17 in × 17 in) when complete and the finished strips are 2.5 cm (1 in) across.

Scatter cushion

Materials
1 m ($1\frac{1}{8}$ yd) of main fabric 90 cm (36 in) wide, including piece for underside of cushion
0.50 m (18 in) of contrast fabric 90 cm (36 in) wide
Unbleached calico or cotton for foundation cloth
47 cm × 47 cm ($18\frac{1}{2}$ in × $18\frac{1}{2}$ in)
Matching zip 35.5 cm (14 in) long
Matching sewing thread

Pattern
Templates are not needed for this pattern but the foundation cloth should be marked with guide-lines to ensure the strips are sewn the correct distance apart. Because this pattern is a little more complicated than the standard *Log Cabin* block, I prefer to mark it in the way shown in figure 86 and use the marks to check the correct position of each strip as it is sewn. Begin by drawing two diagonals from corner to corner on the foundation cloth. The centre point is where the diagonals cross. Around this centre point, draw a 7.5 cm (3 in) square using the fabric weave to keep the lines straight. From the centre of each side of the square, draw lines at right angles to the sides of the square extending out to the edges of the foundation cloth. Along each of these lines, mark seven 2.5 cm (1 in) divisions from the sides of the centre square. Along the diagonal lines mark six 2.5 cm (1 in) divisions from the corners of the centre square. All these divisions should be short 1 cm ($\frac{5}{8}$ in) lines at right angles to the appropriate line except the last division on the diagonals. This should extend to the edges of the foundation fabric to represent the line for the corner triangles.

Cutting out
From main fabric, cut piece 46 cm × 46 cm (18 in × 18 in) for underside of cushion. Cut or tear remaining main fabric into 4 cm ($1\frac{1}{2}$ in) strips. Cut or tear five strips of contrast fabric 90 cm (36 in) long and 4 cm ($1\frac{1}{2}$ in) wide. From remaining contrast fabric cut 9 cm ($3\frac{1}{2}$ in) square for centre and two 21.5 cm ($8\frac{1}{2}$ in) squares. Fold the two large squares diagonally and cut along fold to give four corner triangles. Press all fabric pieces before sewing.

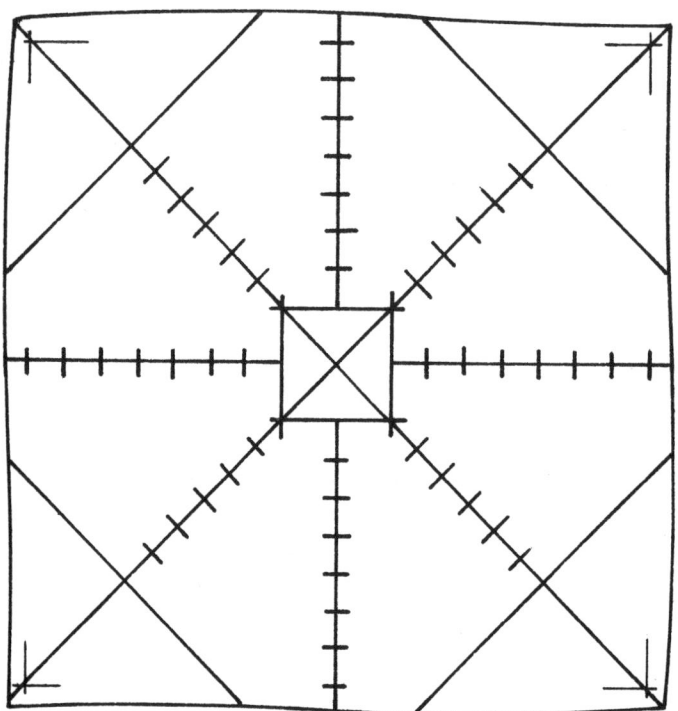

86 Marking foundation cloth for *Pineapple* pattern

87 Piecing first rounds of *Pineapple* pattern on marked foundation cloth

— — — Line for piecing next round

To make up

1 Place centre square in position on foundation fabric allowing raw edges to overlap pencil lines by 7 mm ($\frac{1}{4}$ in). Pin.

2 Using main fabric, sew strips two, three, four and five in position on the four sides of the centre square overlapping previous strip by 6 mm ($\frac{1}{4}$ in) at the corners of the square. Check the accurate position of each strip by measuring in 2.5 cm (1 in) from first division on appropriate line. Cut away surplus after each strip is sewn, turn over and pin.

3 Using contrast fabric, sew strips six, seven, eight and nine diagonally across the first strips of main fabric at the corners of the centre square. Position each of these strips very carefully ensuring that the strip runs at right angles to the appropriate diagonal line. The seam lines for these strips should pass through the corners of the centre square. Cut away surplus after each strip is sewn, turn over and pin.

4 Sew second round of main fabric strips (ten, eleven, twelve and thirteen) parallel to first round and 2.5 cm (1 in) in from second guide-line. Ensure they overlap the previous contrast strips completely. Cut away surplus, turn over and pin.

5 Sew second round of contrast strips parallel to the first round and 2.5 cm (1 in) in from second guide-line on appropriate diagonal line.

6 Continue in this way until seven rounds of main fabric strips and six rounds of contrast strips have been sewn. Complete the patchwork by adding the four corner contrast triangles in the correct position.

7 Finish cushion by attaching zip and completing side seams as in Floor Cushion (page 94).

See colour plate facing page 73
The bedspread is made in the *Straight Furrow* pattern, a
variation of *Log Cabin*. It is made up of fifty-six blocks, each
block is made in an identical manner but turned to the
appropriate position when the blocks are finally pieced
together. It is finished with two borders, lined and tied and,
finally, the binding strip attached around the edge. Although
this bedspread may look a complicated and tricky piece of
work the patchwork is, in fact, simple.
The completed size of the bedspread is 229 cm × 254 cm
(90 in × 100 in) and should cover a standard 137 cm (4 ft 6 in)
double bed. Each finished block is 25.4 cm (10 in) square with
a centre square of 2.5 cm (1 in) and six rows of strips each
2 cm ($\frac{3}{4}$ in) in width.

Bedspread

Materials
4.50 m (5 yd) of assorted light fabrics and 4.50 m (5 yd) of
assorted dark fabrics for the patchwork. A minimum of four
light and four dark fabrics should be used
5.50 m (6 yd) of calico or white cotton for foundation fabric
2.50 m ($2\frac{3}{4}$ yd) cotton sheeting 229 cm (90 in) wide for lining
3 m ($3\frac{1}{3}$ yd) of plain fabric for first border, binding strip and
centres of each block
2.6 m (3 yd) of patterned fabric for second border (half this
amount will do if you piece the border strips)

Pattern
The *Log Cabin* pattern does not require templates but does
require the foundation fabric marking out. After cutting fifty-
six squares of foundation cloth each 30 cm (12 in) square,
follow the instructions given on page 68 for marking *Log
Cabin* blocks but add an extra row of strips. The marked
fabric should have a centre square of 2.5 cm (1 in) and six
rows of 19 mm ($\frac{3}{4}$ in) strips. All fifty-six blocks should be
marked out in this way.

Cutting out
Cut or tear patchwork fabrics into 4 cm ($1\frac{1}{2}$ in) wide strips
and press before using. It saves space and unnecessary
wastage if you cut two strips from each fabric to begin with
then cut more as required. From plain fabric cut fifty-six 4 cm
($1\frac{1}{2}$ in) squares for centres of blocks, four strips 203 cm ×
13 cm (80 in × 5 in) for first border and four strips 259 cm ×
6.5 cm (102 in × 2$\frac{1}{2}$ in) for binding strips.
From patterned fabric for second border cut four strips
259 cm × 10 cm (102 in × 4 in).

To make up

1 Following the instructions given on page 85 for piecing a *Log Cabin* block, make each of the fifty-six blocks in an identical manner by using light fabrics for the first two strips in each round and dark fabrics for the next two strips – see figure 88 for order of piecing. Make sure you have six rounds of strips in each completed block.

2 Lay out completed blocks in position with seven blocks across the width and eight down the length. Position the light and dark sides of each block so they form the contrasting diagonal stripes across the patchwork.

3 Piece blocks together in strips then join the strips together to complete the patchwork.

4 Add plain border by following instructions on page 89 for mitred borders.

5 Add patterned border in the same manner.

6 Attach lining by laying patchwork out on a flat surface, wrong side uppermost. Place lining fabric on top, right side uppermost, and smooth two layers carefully together. Pin together and sew rows of long tacking stitches down and across the work at intervals of approximately 30 cm (12 in) to hold two layers together.

7 Sew binding strip along all edges, following instructions on page 92.

8 Tie lining to patchwork by sewing 1 cm ($\frac{3}{8}$ in) row of satin stitches on lining side holding the lining to the seam allowance of the patchwork at the corners of each block.

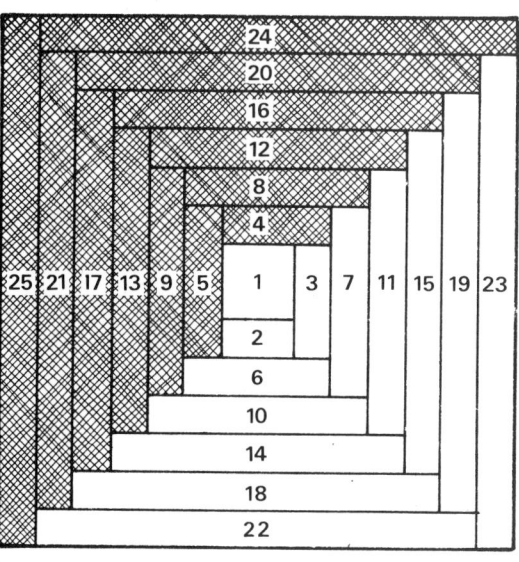

88 Piecing order for each block in bedspread

The skirt shows one attractive way patchwork borders can be used. The skirt illustrated is made in needlecord in plain colours but any fabrics, plain or patterned, could be used. The instructions given are for a 66 cm (26 in) waist and length of 73 cm (28¾ in). To adjust for other sizes, lengthen or shorten main body piece and gather waist to fit appropriate size. Make waistband to fit waist measurement by adding or subtracting patchwork squares.

Skirt with patchwork borders

Materials required
2.50 m (3 yd) of fabric A for main body of skirt and patchwork borders
0.50 m (½ yd) of fabric B for patchwork borders
0.25 m (¼ yd) each of fabrics C and D for wide patchwork border
1.50 m (1¾ yd) of lining fabric 90 cm (36 in) wide
Matching zip 18 cm (7 in) long
Hooks and eyes
Matching sewing thread

Templates
Make templates for square and rectangle shapes by tracing outlines in figure 89. Cut out and mount on sandpaper or stiff card.

Cutting out
For main body of skirt, cut from fabric A:
1 Strip 8 cm wide × 71 cm (3 in × 28 in) long for waistband facing. Adjust if required to fit waist measurement.
2 A piece 47 cm × 145 cm (18½ in × 57 in) for main body of skirt.
3 A strip 5 cm × 145 cm (2 in × 57 in) to place between patchwork borders.
4 A strip 13 cm × 145 cm (5 in × 57 in) for base and hem.
For patchwork, cut eighty-three squares and forty-two rectangles from each of fabrics A and B (add or subtract squares for a larger or smaller waistband). Cut forty-two rectangles from each of fabrics C and D. Allow 7 mm (¼ in) seam allowance around all shapes.

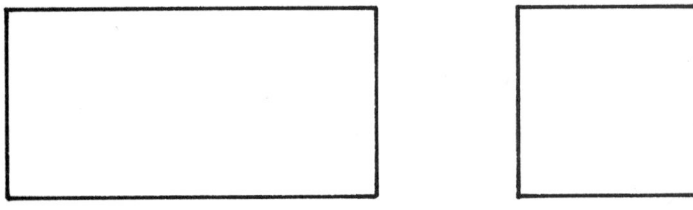

89   Outline of shapes for skirt

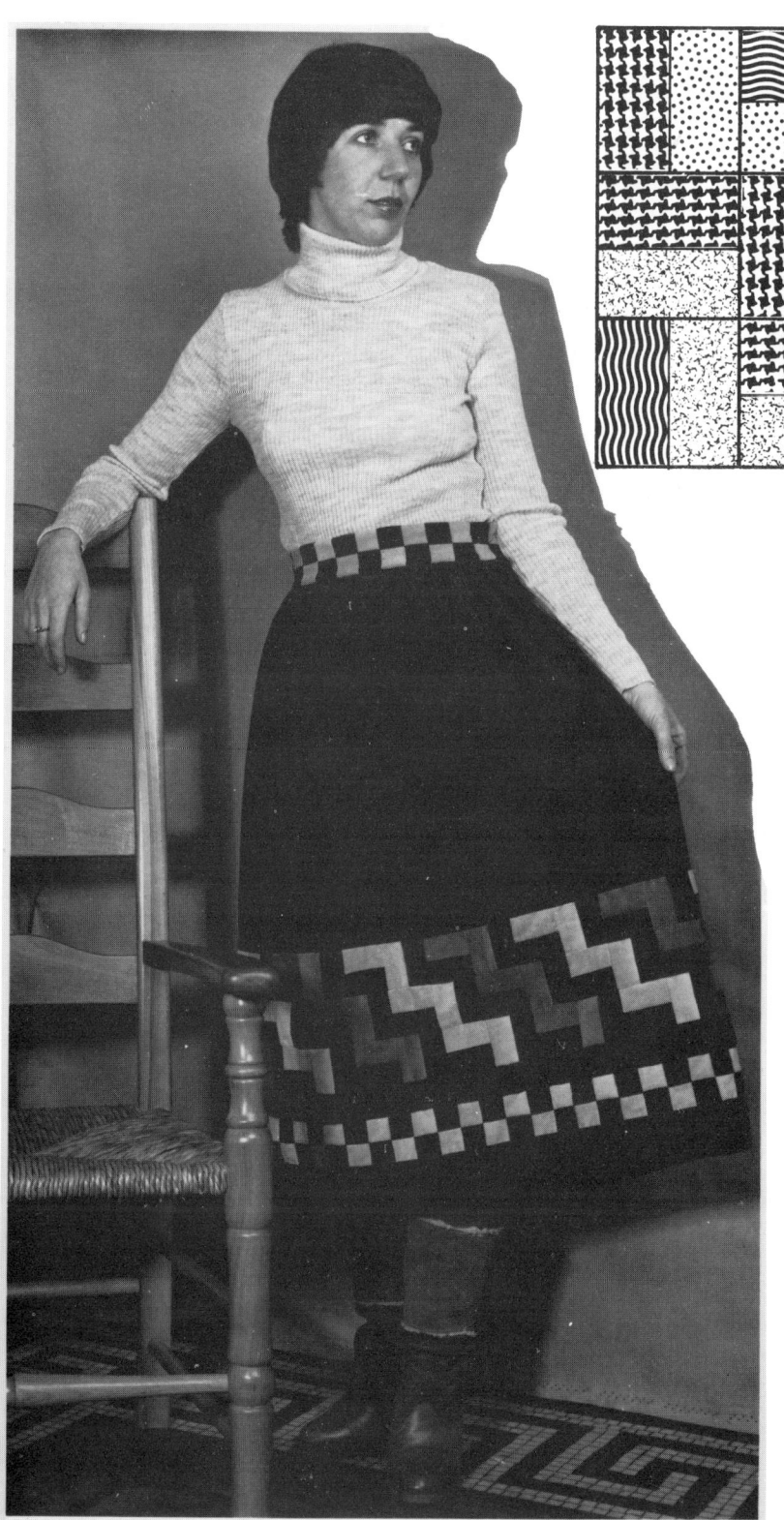

90 Basic pattern unit for deep
border

To make up

1 Begin by joining each square of fabric A to a square of fabric B to produce rectangular patchwork units. Press all seams to the darker colour.

2 Join fifty-six of these rectangular units in a long strip to make the lower patchwork border, alternating the fabrics to produce the checkerboard pattern.

3 Join the remaining rectangular units together in the same way to form the waistband.

4 Piece the main patchwork border by joining together six rectangles of each fabric (A, B, C and D) in the positions indicated in figure 90 to form the basic pattern unit. The rectangles are joined first into 5 cm (2 in) squares, the squares then joined into strips and then the three strips combined to make the pattern unit.

5 Repeat the basic pattern unit six times then join the seven units together to form a long patchwork strip ensuring the correct repeat of the pattern. Press.

6 Join main patchwork border to lower end of main skirt section using flat seam. Press.

7 Add narrow strip of fabric A to lower edge of main patchwork border using flat seam. Press.

8 Add lower patchwork border then add base strip using flat seams. Press.

9 Turn up hem to give base strip a finished depth of 5 cm (2 in) and hem into position.

10 Complete waistband by attaching waistband facing to patchwork waistband strip with a flat seam. Press.

11 Sew up centre back seam to within 20 cm (8 in) of waist. Insert zip.

12 Sew up centre back seam of lining to within 20 cm (8 in) of waist. Tack lining to inside of skirt at waist edge.

13 Mark centre front of skirt and halfway between centre front and centre back, mark positions of left side and right side. Measure 6 cm (2½ in) either side of centre front and centre back and mark with pins. Measure 5 cm (2 in) either side of left and right side and mark with pins. Run line of gathering stitches between these pins. Gather in to fit waistband.

14 With right sides together, attach waistband to skirt machining along patchwork edge. Sew waistband ends. Turn and hand-sew waistband into position on wrong side. Attach hooks and eyes in correct positions. Hand-sew lining into position around zip and finish hem of lining.

Sources of ideas

Once you have mastered the technique of patchwork, you may wish to pursue the craft further and look around for inspiration and stimulus.

The first step is to look at what has been done before. There are several well-illustrated books which trace the history of patchwork, and patchwork quilts in particular, in much greater detail than I have been able to do here. Even though much pre-twentieth century patchwork was sewn by hand, many of the pattern ideas can be easily pieced by machine.

Go to exhibitions of patchwork and patchwork quilts if any come to your area. There is no substitute for looking at the real thing – it can tell you so much more about how the patchwork has been made and, indeed, how well it has been made, than any book illustration. The museum in your area may have some examples of patchwork in its collection. Enquire first and, if necessary, make an appointment. However, it may be that collections not on display can only be made available to serious students. Museum curators are, contrary to popular belief, very busy people and cannot always spare the time to show around anyone with little more than a passing interest.

Having become familiar with traditional patchwork, you may decide to stay within this framework and explore the hundreds of patterns which have been used for decades. Providing one does not slavishly copy another piece of work, I see no reason why traditional patchwork should not be as rewarding and attractive as original work. I see no purpose in encouraging originality for its own sake. One could spend a lifetime exploring traditional pattern possibilities and still not exhaust them.

However, for those who wish to move away from traditional patchwork patterns, there are several areas which would provide stimulus and ideas. The various patterns, forms and colours in nature have always and will always be an endless source of inspiration to artists and craftsmen alike. But the man-made environment, too, can be a source of ideas – brick patterns, tile patterns, furniture decoration, stained glass and mosaics – these and other decorative ideas can often be adapted and translated into patchwork.

Perhaps the best stimulus of all is to establish contact with other people who share your interest in patchwork. This could be done by subscribing to a specialist magazine such as the Quilters' Newsletter, published in the USA, which will keep you up-to-date with current trends and happenings. In Great Britain, the Quilt Circle Newsletter fulfils a similar function. This group also organises workshops, seminars and competitions. Regional craft groups may have members who do patchwork and quilting – the Federation of British Craft Societies can provide a list of such groups. You may find your local Education Authority organises patchwork classes in your area.

It is of enormous value to be able to see the work of other people, to discuss technical details and to share information about fabrics and supplies. It is often possible for a group to club together for supplies – an obvious benefit. This contact between members is an important element in the development of any craft and patchwork has much to gain from a lively exchange of ideas. That such contact is now possible is, perhaps, the most concrete result of the renewed interest in the craft.

Book list

New Discoveries in American Quilts, Robert Bishop, Dutton, 1975

Creative Quilting, Elsa Brown, Pitman, London; Watson Guptill, New York, 1975

Patchwork, Averil Colby, Batsford, London; Branford, Newton Centre, Massachusetts, 1958

Quilting, Averil Colby, Batsford, London; Scribners, New York, 1972

Old Patchwork Quilts, Ruth Finlay, Branford, Massachusetts, 1929

Traditional Quilting, Mavis FitzRandolph, Batsford, 1954

The Perfect Patchwork Primer, Beth Gutcheon, Penguin, London; Viking Penguin, New York, 1973

The Quilt Design Workbook, Beth and Jeffrey Gutcheon, Rawson Associates, 1976

The Pieced Quilt, Jonathan Holstein, New York Graphic Society, 1976

The Standard Book of Quilt-Making and Collecting, Marguerite Ickis, Constable, London; Dover, New York, 1949

Discovering Patchwork, Rosamund Richardson and Erica Griffiths, BBC, 1977

Quiltmaking: The Modern Approach to a Traditional Craft, Ann-Sargent Wooster, Studio Vista, London; Drake Inc, New York, 1974

Ideas for Patchwork, Suzy Ives, Batsford, London, 1974

Patterns for Patchwork Quilts and Cushions, Suzy Ives, Batsford, London, 1977

Useful addresses

Places to visit
The American Museum
Claverton Manor
Bath
Somerset

The Bowes Museum
Barnard Castle
County Durham

Cheltenham City Museum
Clarence Street
Cheltenham
Gloucestershire

Gawthorpe Hall
Padiham
Nr Burnley
Lancashire

North of England Open Air Museum
Beamish
Nr Stanley
County Durham

Ulster Folk Museum
Cultra
Belfast
Northern Ireland

Victoria and Albert Museum
South Kensington
London SW7

Welsh Folk Museum
St Fagan's
Cardiff
Wales

Suppliers of patchwork and quilting requirements
Laura Ashley (fabrics)
30 Great Oak Street
Llanidloes
Powys
Wales

Craftsman's Mark Limited
Broadlands
Shortheath
Farnham
Surrey

Jacob Cowen & Sons Ltd
(terylene wadding in rolls over 40 m)
Ellers Mill
Dalston
Carlisle

J. E. M. Patchwork Templates
Watlington
Oxfordshire, and
Forge House
18 St Helen's Street
Cockermouth
Cumberland

Juniper Supplies (fabrics)
21 Trevor Place
London SW7

Mace and Nairn
89 Crane Street
Salisbury
Wilts

Strawberry Fayre
(fabrics, quilting requirements, etc)
Stockbridge
Hampshire

Other useful addresses
Quilt Circle
c/o Secretary
Flat 8
20 Queens Road
Tunbridge Wells
Kent

Quilter's Newsletter
Box 394
Wheatridge
Colorado 80033
USA

Federation of British Craft Societies
43 Earlham Street
London WC2H 9LD

Crafts Advisory Council (publishers, *Crafts* magazine)
12 Waterloo Place
London SW17 4AU

USA

American Crewel Studio
Box 553
Westfield
New Jersey 07091

American Thread Corporation
90 Park Avenue
New York

Bucky King Embroideries Unlimited
121 South Drive
Pittsburgh
Pennsylvania 15238

Stearns and Foster Company
Quilting department
Cincinnati
Ohio 45215

The Thread Shed
307 Freeport Road
Pittsburgh
Pennsylvania 15215

Yarncrafts Limited
3146 M Street
North West Washington DC

Index

Words in *italics* refer to patchwork patterns
Figures in *italics* refer to illustration numbers

118